Other Books by Devin Brown

The Christian World of The Hobbit

Hobbit Lessons

*Tolkien: How an Obscure Oxford Professor Wrote
The Hobbit and Became the Most Beloved Author of
the Century*

Lessons from the Other Side of the Wardrobe

BRINGING
NARNIA
HOME

DEVIN BROWN

Abingdon Press

Nashville

BRINGING NARNIA HOME
LESSONS FROM THE OTHER SIDE OF THE WARDROBE

Copyright © 2015 by Devin Brown

Library of Congress Cataloging-in-Publication Data has been requested.

ISBN 978-1-4267-91628

Scripture quotations marked NASB are taken from the *New American Standard Bible®*, Copyright © 1960, 1962, 1963, 1968, 1971, 1972, 1973, 1975, 1977, 1995 by The Lockman Foundation. Used by permission. (www.Lockman.org)

Scripture quotations marked NIV are taken from the Holy Bible, NEW INTERNATIONAL VERSION®. Copyright © 1973, 1978, 1984 by International Bible Society. All rights reserved throughout the world. Used by permission of International Bible Society.

15 16 17 18 19 20 21 22 23 24—10 9 8 7 6 5 4 3 2 1

MANUFACTURED IN THE UNITED STATES OF AMERICA

*To my students at Asbury University
who help to remind me that the Narnia stories
are still touching lives*

C. S. Lewis
THE CHRONICLES OF NARNIA
in order of each book's publication

The Lion, the Witch and the Wardrobe (1950)
Prince Caspian (1951)
The Voyage of the Dawn Treader (1952)
The Silver Chair (1953)
The Horse and His Boy (1954)
The Magician's Nephew (1955)
The Last Battle (1956)

CONTENTS

Opening Words

In a dramatic scene from *The Silver Chair*, Puddle-glum declares: "I'm going to live like a Narnian, even if there isn't any Narnia!"

Fortunately, there is a Narnia. This magical land lives not only in the pages of the most amazing set of books that ever came from the pen of C. S. Lewis, but also in the hearts of countless readers all over the world. And in declaring his desire to live like a Narnian, Puddleglum speaks for us all.

What might it be like to live like a Narnian?

When we journey to Narnia, we travel alongside Peter, Susan, Edmund, Lucy, Eustace, and Jill. We see what they see, feel what they feel, and experience what they experience. And in the end—we learn what they learn.

When we finish the last page of each adventure and close the book, we do not have to leave Narnia behind. If we bring home the lessons we have learned and apply them in our own lives, we are like a person who returns from a distant country with a magical treasure. Not someone who buries this treasure in the ground where no one will find it, but instead shares it with everyone they meet.

And then the real magic begins.

The more the treasure is shared, the more there is.

SPOILER ALERT: This book is intended to be read after you have finished reading all seven books in *The Chronicles of Narnia*—not to be read in place of them. If you have not already read C. S. Lewis's original books, do so now. You are in for a real treat!

CHAPTER 1

OF MICE AND MINOTAURS

*Actions We See as Small and Insignificant
Can Be Far More Important Than We Realize*

A TALE OF TWO STORIES

Long before *The Chronicles of Narnia*, there was a series of books collectively known as The Hardy Boys—tales of brothers Frank and Joe Hardy, Bayport High School students by day, solvers of unsolvable mysteries on evenings and weekends. Beginning with *The Tower Treasure*, published in 1927, the teen sleuths have thrilled readers down through the years as they track crooks across town and across the country and bring a long list of thieves, smugglers, kidnappers, spies, bank robbers, and other villains to justice.

The problem with this type of book is that while we find pleasure in reading it, we always return to our own world feeling as though our own lives can never measure up. Unlike Frank and Joe, we will never catch the uncatchable criminal, crack the uncrackable case, cross the uncrossable river, or ride the unrideable pony. We run to this book to escape the hum-drum of ordinary life, but then afterward we return to a world and to lives in this world that have been made a little less wonderful than before.

The unwritten rule for this kind of book is that the main characters—whether they are the Hardy boys or their female counterpart, Nancy Drew—must always be doing something exciting. Not a chapter goes by without something thrilling, suspenseful, or just simply big taking place and our heroes reacting in ways that are equally thrilling and big. And the people they encounter while doing these big things are big as well—an eclectic mix of the famous and infamous.

And so we long to be one of the Hardy brothers or Nancy Drew. We imagine ourselves standing in their shoes and rescuing the trapped victim, finding the stolen loot, foiling the bad guys' plots, and making the world safe again.

The problem is that in our own lives we rarely if ever do anything big—not big in the Hardy Boys sense. What we seem to do are lots of small things. And stories like The Hardy Boys leave us feeling as though doing small things is not something that is all that important. We turn to this type of book because our own lives do not seem very exciting, and what we find there makes our day-to-day life seem even duller.

Fortunately, there is another type of book that helps remind us of our significance in the grand plan and makes the events of our lives—the things we do and the people we do them with—more special, not less. Yes, this type of book also creates a longing in us, but it is a very different sort of longing than we get with the first kind. C. S. Lewis suggests that the reader of this kind of book does not despise real woods because he has read about enchanted ones; the reading makes all real woods a little bit enchanted. Rather than making the real world seem duller, this other type of book gives our world what Lewis calls a new dimension of depth.

All seven works in *The Chronicles of Narnia* are perfect examples of this second type of book and serve as reminders that actions we may see as small and insignificant can be far more important than we realize. Let's look at some places where Lewis explores this principle.

SUSAN AND LUCY MAKE A HUGE DIFFERENCE

One of the most dramatic scenes in all of the Chronicles takes place about two-thirds of the way through *The Lion, the Witch and the Wardrobe* when Aslan arrives at the Stone Table to give his life in exchange for Edmund's. A menacing crowd waits for him in the torch light—ogres, hags, bull-headed men, and other evil creatures best left unnamed. And right in the middle is the White Witch.

Everyone remembers what happens next as Aslan, without offering any resistance, allows himself to be bound and shaved and finally to be killed. Everyone remembers the marvelous events that take place the next morning when, with a great crack, the Stone Table breaks in two and Aslan appears alive once more, shining in the sunrise and shaking his mane.

What people may not remember as well is the tender scene that takes place on the way to the Stone Table.

If you were to ask Susan and Lucy about it, they would say it all began when neither of them could sleep because of a terrible feeling they had about Aslan. This feeling gets so bad they decide to get up and see if they can find him—and they do. On the far side of the campground they notice Aslan walking slowly into the woods, looking as if he is very tired and deep in thought.

On and on in the pale moonlight, the girls silently follow the great lion. Finally, as they are crossing an open space, Aslan turns around and sees them. When Susan begs to be allowed to go with him, Aslan makes a surprising response.

"I should be glad of company tonight," he tells

them, but he makes it clear they will have to stop when he tells them and let him go on alone.

I should be glad of company tonight. It seems odd that the king of the wood, the son of the great Emperor-beyond-the-Sea, should need company— particularly the company of two ordinary schoolgirls from Finchley.

Forward they go again with one girl on each side. "But how slowly he walked!" Lewis tells us. Aslan's great royal head droops so that his nose nearly touches the grass. Presently he stumbles and gives a low moan.

When Lucy and Susan ask what is wrong and if he is ill, Aslan replies, "No, I am sad and lonely." And then comes one of the most touching moments in the entire series. The great lion asks the girls to lay their hands on his mane so he can feel they are there. The girls bury their hands in the beautiful sea of fur and stroke it, and so they continue on to the Stone Table.

Now if you asked Susan and Lucy what they had done on that sad, lonely night, they probably would say they didn't do anything much. They just walked with Aslan and kept their hands on his mane so he would know they were with him.

But if you asked Aslan about that same night, he would say that having Susan and Lucy there meant all the world to him. He would say that what they did made all the difference. They never left his side—

not for a second. They always kept their hands on his mane. He was not alone.

And so the first lesson we bring home from Narnia is this: actions we see as small and insignificant can be far more important than we realize. This is true for kind and loving actions; it also is true for actions that are not kind and not loving.

"Go On, Edmund, Tell Them All about It"

The Lion, the Witch and the Wardrobe begins during the London air raids of World War II, as the four Pevensie children are sent to stay at the house of an old professor. While exploring on the first day, Lucy enters a mysterious wardrobe. The problem comes when no one will believe her story of how she was magically transported to the land of Narnia and met a faun named Mr. Tumnus, who invited her to tea.

Several days later during a game of hide-and-seek, Lucy again enters the wardrobe, and Edmund follows shortly afterward. While Lucy visits Mr. Tumnus again, Edmund meets up with the White Witch, who puts him under her spell and has him promise he will return to her castle with his siblings. Lucy comes upon Edmund just moments after the Witch drives off, and together they journey back through the wardrobe to the professor's house.

Excited that her brother now can corroborate her

story, Lucy immediately finds Peter and Susan. "Go on, Edmund," she says. "Tell them all about it."

At this point Lewis breaks in to warn readers. "And now," he cautions, "we come to one of the nastiest things in this story."

Fans of *The Lion, the Witch and the Wardrobe* know that there are a number of nasty things that take place over the course of the story. Innocent creatures, including poor Mr. Tumnus, get turned to stone. Edmund keeps his promise to the White Witch and betrays his sisters and brother. Worst of all is the grim scene already mentioned where Aslan is sacrificed at the Stone Table.

So what is this terrible thing that comes next, something that will be one of the nastiest things in the story? Edmund simply decides to tell a lie about his trip to Narnia and says that he and Lucy were just pretending. Surely one little lie won't matter much. But Lewis does not see it as one little lie. He sees it as one of the nastiest things that happens in the book.

Again we see that actions we may think of as small and insignificant—whether good or bad—can be far more important than we realize.

Bringing Narnia Home

In the final chapters of *The Lion, the Witch and the Wardrobe*, the White Witch is defeated, and Peter,

Susan, Edmund, and Lucy are crowned kings and queens at Cair Paravel. During the years they reign over Narnia, Lucy becomes known as "Lucy the Valiant." And in giving Lucy this title, Lewis makes it clear that courage is not limited to the battlefield— that someone can be valiant through what might seem to be small actions.

In *Prince Caspian*, the story that follows, we meet the great-hearted mouse Reepicheep, who is gravely wounded in the final combat against Miraz's troops. Lucy is able to use her magic cordial to heal him but not to restore his severed tail. When Reepicheep appeals to Aslan for his assistance, the great lion agrees, not for the sake of Reepicheep's honor, as he tells the gallant mouse, but for "the kindness your people showed me long ago when you ate away the cords that bound me on the Stone Table." And here when Aslan says long ago, he really means it— as *Prince Caspian* takes place over thirteen hundred years after the events in *The Lion, the Witch and the Wardrobe*.

From Lucy and Susan's walk with Aslan, to Edmund's lie about going to Narnia, to the mice who nibble away the cords that bind Aslan and whose deeds are remembered down through the centuries, Lewis reminds us that actions we see as small and insignificant can be far more important than we realize.

"Further In"

Questions for Reflection

1. Can you think of other times in *The Chronicles of Narnia* when actions that may not have seemed particularly big or spectacular at the time turned out to be important? What events or circumstances do you recall?

2. From your own life, can you think of something someone did for you that might not have made headlines but made all the difference to you? Try to remember some of the details. How did this person's generosity make you feel at the time? Or was it only later that you began to realize the importance of it to you?

3. Can you think of something you yourself have done that did not seem like something big at the time, but which you later realized was a big thing?

CHAPTER 2

DESPITE WHAT WHITE WITCHES, TISROCS, AND OTHER PETTY TYRANTS THINK

Being a Leader Means More Than Simply Being the Boss

SHE CALLS HERSELF THE QUEEN OF NARNIA

Early in chapter 4 of *The Lion, the Witch and the Wardrobe*, we find Edmund sitting in the White Witch's sleigh, her warm mantle tucked snugly around him, shoveling down Turkish Delight as fast as he can. And with each piece of the enchanted candy he consumes, Edmund falls further under the Witch's spell as she entices him with promises of not only more Turkish Delight but of one day ruling Narnia.

"I want a nice boy whom I could bring up as a Prince and who would be King of Narnia when I am gone," the White Witch explains. "While he was

Prince he would wear a gold crown and eat Turkish Delight all day long."

In the Witch's promise to make Edmund king of Narnia after she is gone, there are two points worth noting. First, the Witch is immortal unless killed in battle, and so her promise here to make Edmund king after she is gone is all a lie. She has no plans to *ever* be gone.

Second, her plan is actually a false imitation of Aslan's plan for Edmund. In fact, Edmund is *supposed* to rule as a king of Narnia—the prophecy related by Mr. Beaver makes this clear. However, Aslan's conception of being a king or queen involves far more than wearing a golden crown and sitting around all day eating Turkish Delight.

In *The Magician's Nephew*, Uncle Andrew's magic rings allow Digory and Polly to travel to another world where they meet up with the White Witch *before* she becomes the White Witch—back when she was known as Jadis, the last Queen of Charn. They learn that just as she was about to be defeated, she had spoken the Deplorable Word, which destroyed all living beings in her world except her. When Digory and Polly express horror at the thought of all the people who were destroyed, Jadis matter-of-factly replies: "I was the Queen. They were all *my* people. What else were they there for but to do my will?"

Earlier, the Witch had taken no notice of Polly because Digory was the one she wanted to make use of. Lewis then jumped in to explain: "I expect most witches are like that. They are not interested in things or people unless they can use them."

The White Witch is a tyrant, and her insatiable craving for control is the trait that most clearly defines her. We could say she is obsessed by her need to dominate everything and everybody, and because of this she can never rest. She is always on the offensive, always looking to bring everyone else into submission. For her, and for tyrants like her, being the king or queen means being the boss. And that is *all* it means.

Throughout the Narnia stories, Lewis shows us two rival conceptions of what it means to govern. One side—whether it's the White Witch, Miraz, the Green Lady, or Shift the Ape—sees being a ruler as simply a means of controlling others and using them to get whatever they want. Aslan's idea of what it means to be a ruler is radically different.

MY SUBJECTS OR MY SCHOOLMASTERS

The last few chapters of *The Voyage of the Dawn Treader* take on an almost dreamlike quality as the ship draws closer and closer to the end of the world. After several days where they glide on a smooth sea of lilies, the water gradually becomes shallower and shallower, and finally the time comes when the *Dawn Treader* can sail no further east. Caspian calls for a small boat to be lowered and orders the crew to gather for an important announcement. It is Eustace—perhaps because he himself once lived a life of doing only what he pleased—who first notices a strange look in Caspian's eyes, a look that causes the young king to appear, as the narrator points out, not unlike his uncle Miraz.

Caspian tells the crew that with the seven lords now accounted for and Reepicheep sworn to remain at the end of the world and thus undo the sleepers' enchantment, they have now fulfilled their quest. He instructs Drinian to bring the ship and crew safely back to Narnia and, once there, to have Trumpkin pay out the rewards that were promised. Finally, should he himself fail to return, Caspian tells them, they must select a new king.

When Drinian interrupts to ask if Caspian is abdicating, the young king declares that he has decided to go with Reepicheep to see the World's End. Reepicheep is quick to point out Caspian's mistake, telling him: "You break faith with all your subjects, and especially with Trumpkin."

Caspian's announced intention of going with Reepicheep to see World's End is not a terrible desire.

In fact, this same longing in Reepicheep takes on a noble and heroic quality. So exactly what is it that causes Caspian for a moment to look like his Uncle Miraz?

Caspian's resemblance to his evil uncle stems not from his desire to see the end of the world but from the fact that here Caspian *will not be told that he cannot do something*. Briefly, and it is only for a moment, Caspian sees kingship as meaning only that he can do what he wants when he wants, and no one can stop him.

In words that could have been said by his uncle, Caspian complains, "I had thought you were all my subjects here, not my schoolmasters." His hand is on his sword, threatening violence, when Lucy intervenes to remind him that he has almost promised Ramandu's daughter he would return. Even then, Caspian is still in a temper at having his orders questioned and declares: "Well, have your way. The quest is ended. We all return." In fact, this is not an acceptable solution, for if they leave no one behind, the sleepers' enchantment will not be broken. Again Reepicheep dares to defy the king, saying: "We do not *all* return."

At this Caspian cries, "Will no one silence that Mouse?" and storms into his cabin and slams the door.

When the others join the king a short time later, they find him greatly changed. Through his tears Caspian explains that Aslan had appeared, a bit stern at first, and had told him that Reepicheep, Edmund, Lucy, and Eustace are to go on alone and the others must turn back at once.

Although Caspian is compared to Miraz in this scene, his intentions here are not inherently evil. Miraz had murdered the rightful king, Caspian's father, and taken his crown; Caspian only wants to go to the end of the world. But while this might be a very good thing to do, Caspian has responsibilities that prohibit him from doing so. Reepicheep points out to him, "You shall not please yourself with adventures as if you were a private person."

A king may not please himself as if he were a private person. The same goes for a queen and for anyone in charge. Lewis's point is that in Narnia, as well as in our own world, being a leader means more than simply being the boss. A lot more.

FIRST IN THE CHARGE, LAST IN THE RETREAT

Near the end of *The Magician's Nephew*, Aslan tells Frank and Helen, a London cabby and his equally astonished wife, that they are to be the first king and queen of Narnia. He explains that they are to rule and do justice among the animals of Narnia and to protect them from their enemies.

Aslan asks, "Can you rule these creatures kindly and fairly, remembering that they are not slaves like the dumb beasts of the world you were born in, but Talking Beasts and free subjects?" Aslan's point about ruling with kindness and fairness is critical. His statement that those being ruled are *not slaves* but *free subjects* is exactly what the White Witch fails to understand.

Aslan concludes his summary of what it means to properly govern with a final question: "And if enemies came against the land…would you be the first in the charge and the last in the retreat?" In other words, leaders have to be more concerned for those they rule than for themselves. Lewis has King Lune echo this same point in *The Horse and His Boy*. Rather than enjoying a position of endless privilege, Lune explains to Shasta that a king must be "first in every desperate attack and last in every desperate retreat."

King Miraz, Caspian's wicked uncle, follows the reverse principle, as his general rule is to be last in the charge and first in the retreat. It is only after his courtiers suggest he is too old and weak to fight, that Miraz agrees to face Peter in single combat, and then only because his vanity is injured, not because he wants to spare his army a gruesome battle.

In *The Horse and His Boy*, upon hearing the news that his brother Cor (Shasta) is the rightful heir to the throne, Corin cries out, "Hurrah! I shan't have to be King."

Why such happiness at learning he will *not* be the next ruler? As Corin declares from firsthand experience, "It's princes have all the fun." Or as Lewis would say, it's kings who have all the work and responsibility.

BRINGING NARNIA HOME

If, as we have seen, in Narnia being a leader means more than simply being the boss, then we should not be surprised when those given the task of leading sometimes show reluctance in assuming the role.

When Aslan asks Caspian if he feels sufficient to take up the kingship of Narnia, the young prince haltingly answers: "I—I don't think I do, Sir. I'm only a kid."

In the same vein, when King Frank is asked the question of whether as a ruler he would be first in the charge and last in the retreat, the former cabby can only say: "I'd try—that is, I 'ope I'd try—to do my bit."

And both these answers are good enough for Aslan.

"FURTHER IN"

QUESTIONS FOR REFLECTION

1. Can you think of other examples of leaders in Narnia—good ones who try to serve their subjects or bad ones who view their subjects as their slaves?

2. Drawing from your own personal experience, can you think of someone who was a particularly good leader? What made this person a good leader? Can you think of someone who was a poor leader? What was it that made this person a poor leader?

3. Finally, what about yourself? When have you had to be a leader? What was the hardest thing about it?

CHAPTER 3

BAD *CAN* BE BEAUTIFUL

(At Least on the Surface)

HE CALLED HIMSELF LORD PROTECTOR

One of the most important scenes in *Prince Caspian* is one that Lewis leaves to our imagination. Picture a funeral service in a darkened hall. Despite her grief, the widow stands with quiet dignity alongside the royal coffin. Holding her hand in the flickering torch light is a small boy too young to fully understand what has happened. A tall, commanding man—whose face resembles that of the deceased and suggests they were close relatives—offers comfort and condolences.

The widow is the wife of Caspian the Ninth, whose body now lies in state. The boy is their only child, a very young Prince Caspian. The tall man is the late king's brother and the boy's uncle. His name is Miraz.

"When he first began to rule, he did not even

pretend to be the King," Doctor Cornelius will explain to the Prince much later. "He called himself Lord Protector."

Lord Protector: The title suggests that its owner is assuming power only temporarily and only in order to *protect* the rightful king until he is older and can rule the kingdom himself. And so, Miraz becomes one of Lewis's best illustrations of the principle that a person can look fair on the surface and be foul underneath—a reminder that evil often comes disguised as good.

In the weeks and months following the funeral, one by one, all the great lords who had been faithful to the former king die or disappear under strange circumstances. Finally there are only seven left, and these are "persuaded" by Miraz to sail beyond the Eastern Ocean, supposedly to search for new lands. As Miraz intended, they never return and so become the seven lost lords that Caspian will go in search of in *The Voyage of the Dawn Treader*.

Even after all of his brother's supporters are eliminated, Miraz does not simply seize the throne. That would be too direct, too obvious. Miraz has his flatterers beg him to become king in order to make it seem as though he does so only reluctantly and only out of a deep sense of duty.

Soon the good queen passes away, leaving Caspian in the supposed protection of his uncle. And for a time, King Miraz, as he is now called, cares for his nephew, though in a cold, impersonal way, and only as long as he and his wife have no children of their own. Better that one of his own kin have his throne when he dies than for it to go to one of his lords; at least it stays in the family. But then Miraz and his wife have a son, and any pretense of caring about Caspian is discarded. Once he has his own heir, the former Lord Protector wants Caspian, the rightful heir to the throne, dead.

"Is he really as bad as that?" Caspian asks his tutor. "Would he really murder me?"

"He murdered your father," Doctor Cornelius replies.

Now, for the first time, Caspian sees his evil uncle for what he truly is. But for many years Caspian was deceived by appearances. For a long time Miraz's evil was disguised as something good.

Harmless or Beautiful Faces

Near the end of *Prince Caspian*, in a chapter entitled "Sorcery and Sudden Vengeance," we find the Old Narnians in desperate straits. After enduring defeat after defeat by Miraz's army, Caspian's council faces real doubts about how much longer they can hold out. Nikabrik has brought in two *friends*, as he calls them, to the council meeting. But exactly who these friends are is not clear, causing Doctor Cornelius—who has had experience with the way evil can be disguised—to be suspicious.

"You there," he says, addressing the more human of the two, "who and what are you?"

In a thin and whining voice, the creature assures them they have no need to be afraid of an old woman who is "nearly doubled up with the rheumatics and hasn't two sticks to put under her kettle." This supposedly harmless old woman with rheumatism turns out to be an evil Hag who nearly kills Doctor Cornelius before Peter, Edmund, and Trumpkin rush in to help.

Some friend.

Besides the mask of a protector, which Miraz wears, and the mask of harmlessness, which the Hag wears, another way evil can be disguised is to hide behind the mask of beauty—and this is the disguise used by the White Witch.

When Digory and Polly journey to Charn in *The Magician's Nephew*, they come to a great room filled with hundreds of people frozen in time, all seated as still as statues. As they walk down the long line, the last figure they come to is that of a woman who has a look on her face of such fierceness and pride it takes their breath away. She is dazzlingly beautiful as well, so beautiful that, even many years later, Digory will still say that he had never in all his life known anyone so beautiful.

This proud, fierce woman is, of course, Jadis, the White Witch. When she reaches London, her disguise of beauty will deceive Uncle Andrew as well. When Edmund meets her in *The Lion, the Witch and the Wardrobe*, we find that it fools him, too.

Within minutes after Edmund's arrival in Narnia, a great sleigh drawn by two reindeer pulls up alongside him. Inside, he sees a great lady, who despite her icy, snow-white complexion is described as very beautiful. In addition to using her beauty, the White Witch also masks her evil intentions with candy and sweet-sounding words. She tells Edmund (who has been stuffing himself with sticky Turkish Delight and at this point is not at all handsome) that he is the cleverest and handsomest young man she has ever met. She asks him to bring Peter, Susan, and Lucy back to her castle—not because they are special, like he is, but so they can be his courtiers. Of course, what the Witch really wants is for Edmund to betray his siblings so that she can kill them and then kill him as well.

Edmund believes the sugary sweet lies that come from the beautiful lady's ruby red lips. He has not— *at this point*—learned how evil can be deceptive and how it may appear to be beautiful on the surface. Later in the story, Edmund will see through the White Witch's appearance. And then the lies he told himself that she was good and kind and that her side was really the right side will sound ridiculous to him.

In yet another example, this one from *The Last Battle*, we find Shift the Ape, who is not beautiful or noble himself, hiding behind the beautiful and noble face of Aslan. Calling himself Aslan's mouthpiece, Shift wants everyone to believe that the selfish orders he gives come not from him but from the great lion himself. In one instance he tells the animals of Narnia, "I want—I mean Aslan wants—some more nuts. These you've brought aren't anything like enough. You must bring some more, do you hear? Twice as many. And they've got to be here by sunset tomorrow, and there mustn't be any bad ones or any small ones among them."

I want—I mean Aslan wants—some more nuts. In the end, the creatures of Narnia finally see through Shift's deception and reject the ape's attempt to rule over them in the name of Aslan, but not before his lies have caused great pain and destruction.

Evil's Most Cunning Deception

Of course evil's most cunning and compelling disguise, the one that is hardest for us to see through, is the mask that our own evil hides behind. In Edmund,

Eustace, and Bree, we find illustrations of the principle that no man—or boy or horse—does evil in his own eyes.

As the four children make their way toward the Lamp-post in *The Lion, the Witch and the Wardrobe*, Edmund briefly forgets that he needs to pretend he has never been there and suggests they should bear a bit more to the left.

After a moment of dead silence Peter exclaims, "Of all the poisonous little beasts!" Then he can say no more as he considers the wickedness of Edmund's lie. While *we* can clearly see that Edmund is in the wrong, Edmund himself cannot. Somehow—and unless we have done this ourselves, it is hard to understand how—Edmund sees *himself* as the injured party and thinks, "I'll pay you all out for this, you pack of stuck-up, self-satisfied prigs."

Later as Edmund is trudging through the snow on his way to the Witch's castle to betray the others, he still refuses to see his actions for what they are. While he does not want the Witch to be as nice to Peter, Susan, or Lucy or to place them on the same level as him, he manages to convince himself that she is not really going to do anything bad to them. Somehow he refuses to see that he is betraying them to her.

And this is how evil works, Lewis suggests. It hides the real truth beneath lies, disguises, and excuses.

Before his transformation into a dragon in *The Voyage of the Dawn Treader*, Eustace has a similar blindness to his own wickedness. We see this blindness in the diary he keeps. There he refers to the others—characters that anyone else would love to be friends with—as fiends in human form and writes that Caspian and Edmund have been "simply brutal" to him. Perhaps Eustace's most outrageous claim is that he always tries to consider others whether they are nice to him or not.

While not as wicked as Edmund or Eustace were, Bree, in *The Horse and His Boy*, is just as blind to his own faults. In Bree's case, his faults are associated with a distorted sense of pride about his appearance. He had been forced to have his tail cut to disguise himself as a work horse. Now, he will not leave the Hermit's and go on to Narnia simply because his tail has not grown out, and Hwin and Aravis rightly accuse him of being as vain and as silly as the Tarkheena they encountered in Tashbaan. Even after his errors are pointed out, Bree refuses to see them and instead claims his hesitation is simply due to a "proper respect" for himself and his fellow horses.

Although the White Witch and Miraz lack any capacity for self-criticism and never see the error of their ways, this is not true for Edmund, Eustace, and Bree as they are led out of their moral blindness by an encounter each of them has with Aslan. Looking back they will be able to see through the lies they told themselves. "Gosh! What a little tick I was," Eustace will later confess. Edmund will tell Eustace, "You haven't been as bad as I was on my first trip to Narnia." And Bree will tell Aslan, "I'm afraid I must be rather a fool."

Aslan's reply to Bree is a fitting reply to all who finally see their flaws and realize that they have been fools in thinking how perfect they are. "Happy the horse who knows that while he is still young," the great lion states. "Or the human either."

BRINGING NARNIA HOME

As we have seen, evil often does not look like evil, but wears a disguise. The question remains: Why would evil not want to appear as it really is?

One reason is because when we see evil as it really is—in ourselves or others—it loses its hold on us. Without its mask, evil is cruel, destructive, and ugly. Unless we have lost all moral sensibility, *to truly see evil is to be repulsed by it and to reject it*.

Because we can see their wickedness (even when they themselves cannot), we like and admire the *later* Edmund and Eustace, not the *earlier* ones. No one in the history of reading *The Chronicles of Narnia* has ever said, "I want be like Edmund when he was betraying his brother and sisters" or "I want to be like Eustace when he was stuck-up and selfish."

About two-thirds of the way through *The Lion, the Witch and the Wardrobe* we find one of Lewis's most dramatic rescue scenes. Edmund has gone from being on the Witch's side to being her hostage and is about to become her victim. She orders him to be bound to a tree and begins to sharpen her Stone Knife. Aslan's forces arrive just in the nick of time, and in the chaos that ensues, the Witch and the dwarf appear to have fled. However, after the rescue party leaves with Edmund, we discover that the Witch has used her power to disguise herself as a boulder and her dwarf assistant as a stump. Then the narrator gives us a key piece of information, as we are told: "It was part of her magic that she could make things look like what they aren't."

And this is exactly Lewis's point: *evil has a power to make itself look like what it isn't*. But by reading *The Chronicles of Narnia*, we can become more aware of how evil can wear a disguise and so become better able to see through it.

"Further In"

Questions for Reflection

1. In this chapter we examined how evil may not appear as evil. Can you think of other evil characters from fairytales who do not appear evil and who disguise their true intentions?

2. In your own life, have you ever met someone who appeared friendly or caring on the surface, but later turned out to be the opposite? What were some of the details of that encounter? What were your feelings when you learned the truth?

3. How about your own actions—have you ever tried to excuse something bad you did? Can you think of an occasion when it was hard for you to see your own flaws?

CHAPTER 4

I THOUGHT WE WERE GETTING *REAL* SOLDIERS!

Sometimes Help Does Not Look Like Help Until Much Later

STRANGE HELP

Deep in the night, Prince Caspian is unexpectedly roused from sleep by Doctor Cornelius. "Put on all your clothes," his tutor says in a hushed whisper. "You have a long journey before you." Caspian dresses quickly and is taken to the top of the Great Tower, a place where no one below can hear what is said.

"Your life is in danger," Doctor Cornelius explains, and then he tells the young prince the full story of how Miraz had killed Caspian's father, stolen Caspian's crown, and now—with the birth of Miraz's own son that night—wants to rid himself of the rightful heir to the throne.

Caspian's tutor gives him a small purse of gold and then, just before sending his pupil out into the world, puts a strange object into his hands: the magic horn of Queen Susan herself.

"It is said that whoever blows it shall have strange help—no one can say how strange," Doctor Cornelius explains. And with one last handclasp and a few tears, Caspian gallops off into the night.

Centuries earlier, when the horn originally was given to Susan in *The Lion, the Witch and the Wardrobe*, it came with this promise from Father Christmas: "When you put this horn to your lips and blow it, then, wherever you are, I think help of some kind will come to you."

Strange help—no one can say how strange. Help of some kind.

Why these odd qualifications on the type of aid the horn will bring? Why *strange* help instead of normal help? Why help of *some* kind instead of help of the ordinary kind? For an answer to these questions, we need to look at what happens when the horn is used.

Lewis reports only two uses of Susan's horn in the Chronicles. In *The Lion, the Witch and the Wardrobe,* when Maugrim, the White Witch's great wolf, attacks Susan, the horn call does not bring a powerful creature from Aslan's army, but only her slightly older brother Peter—someone who has never used a sword or been in a battle before. "Peter did not feel very brave," we are told. "Indeed, he felt he was going to be sick."

However, Peter's fear does not keep him from doing what he has to. He rushes straight up to the great wolf, and after a "horrible, confused moment like something in a nightmare," he manages to slay it. As Susan climbs down from the tree limb she was clinging to and joins Peter on the ground, Lewis concludes, "I won't say there wasn't kissing and crying on both sides."

Kissing and crying. Strange help, indeed.

So why this help *of some kind*? Why help from Peter instead of one of the mighty centaurs standing nearby or even from Aslan himself? With Peter's coming, not only is Susan saved, but the new High King has his first experience in combat. And Peter will need this experience the next day when he must lead his forces into battle against those of the Witch.

The other recorded use of the horn occurs in chapter 7 of *Prince Caspian* as the Old Narnians have reached the end of their ability to hold out against Miraz's forces. "If your Majesty is ever to use the horn," Trufflehunter advises Caspian, "I think the time has now come."

Doctor Cornelius reminds the council that they

do not know what form the help will take. The horn might call Peter the High King and his mighty consorts from the past or even Aslan himself. Nor do they know when or where the help might arrive, so messengers are sent to wait at the Lamp-post and Cair Paravel.

But when the prince blows Susan's magic horn, his call for help is not answered by the great warriors he and his army were hoping for, nor by Aslan, but by the four Pevensie children who are just one year older than on their first visit. Trumpkin, who was sent as one of the messengers, explains to them: "The King and Trufflehunter and Doctor Cornelius were expecting—well, if you see what I mean, help....I think they'd been imagining you as great warriors. As it is—we're awfully fond of children and all that, but just at the moment, in the middle of a war—but I'm sure you understand."

The four children do understand. At first glance they do not look as though they will be much help. But after a fencing match with Edmund, a shooting contest with Susan, and a demonstration of the healing power of Lucy's cordial, Trumpkin admits he has learned his lesson—*help sometimes may not seem like help, especially not at first.*

THE ADVENTURES OF EUSTACE

Strange help appears not only in *The Lion, the Witch and the Wardrobe* and *Prince Caspian* but throughout the Narnia stories. Perhaps the best example of strange help is the peculiar form of assistance that Eustace receives.

"There was a boy called Eustace Clarence Scrubb, and he almost deserved it."

Here we have Lewis's most famous opening line and the beginning of one of his most popular stories—*The Voyage of the Dawn Treader*. We are told that the boy was called Scrubb by his teachers and Eustace Clarence by his parents. Then the narrator adds, "I can't tell you how his friends spoke to him, for he had none."

Why is it that Eustace has no friends? We very quickly discover he is exceptionally proud, selfish, and unpleasant—all of which makes him exceptionally unlovable. But what Eustace is unaware of is that he has someone who does love him and cares enough to help him out of his miserable, friendless state. To us Eustace may seem a lost cause and beyond help, but there is one kind of strange help that will have an effect. Eustace is going to Narnia, and once there he will be turned into a dragon. And what he initially sees as the worst thing that could ever happen to him—being changed into a gruesome monster—will turn out to be the best thing.

About a third of the way into the *Dawn Treader*'s journey to recover the seven lost lords, the crew see a great line of clouds building on the horizon. The sea turns a drab yellow, the air grows cold, and suddenly the storm hits. For thirteen days and nights the crew must fight for their lives before the storm finally subsides. Eventually reaching a seemingly uninhabited island, they put in to resupply and make repairs. All hands are put to work filling water casks, mending sails, and hunting for food—all hands except Eustace's. In addition to being exceptionally proud, selfish, and unpleasant, Eustace is also exceptionally lazy. When no one is watching, he wanders off in search of a cool place in the mountains to have a long (and in his opinion well-earned) sleep.

But soon a fog rolls in, causing Eustace to lose his way. When it finally lifts, he finds himself in an unknown valley and with the sea nowhere in sight. He is not there for long when he witnesses an old dragon crawl from its lair to a pool of water where it dies, nearly at Eustace's feet. Suddenly a peal of thunder and a drenching rain sends Eustace scurrying for the only shelter around— the dragon's cave—where he settles in to wait out the downpour by finally taking his long nap.

When he wakes, Eustace gradually comes to see that something is wrong, terribly wrong. As Lewis tells us, "Sleeping on a dragon's hoard with greedy, dragonish thoughts in his heart, he had become a dragon himself."

Eustace's loathsome exterior now mirrors his vile interior—and he is filled with a series of painful realizations. He realizes that the others had not really been fiends at all, and he begins to see that he had not been as nice a person as he had supposed.

The days that follow are agonizing for Eustace—in part because he had wedged a golden bracelet on his upper arm before turning into a dragon, and now it is cutting into his much larger dragon arm; but mostly because more and more, Eustace comes to see himself as he really is. In the end, Eustace has an encounter with Aslan and, with the great lion's help, is changed back into a boy—the boy he was always meant to be.

"It would be nice," the narrator points out, "and fairly nearly true, to say that 'from that time forth Eustace was a different boy.' To be strictly accurate, he began to be a different boy. He had relapses. There were still many days when he could be very tiresome. But most of these I shall not notice. The cure had begun."

Being changed into a monstrous dragon as the cure for self-centeredness? Strange, but true. Here again we see that *help often comes in a manner that is so unexpected that it may be recognized as help only in looking back on it.*

I Do Not Call You Unfortunate

Near the end of *The Horse and His Boy*, Shasta successfully delivers the warning to King Lune of

Archenland about the enemies approaching from Tashbaan. But in the subsequent race to the capital city of Anvard, Shasta—who has never before ridden any horse but Bree—falls behind and becomes separated from the king and his entourage. Before long he finds himself on the wrong mountain pass—tired, alone, and hungry, and lost in a thick fog—going not toward Anvard but away from it.

"I *do* think," he says, speaking to himself and the non-talking horse he is on, "that I must be the most unfortunate boy that ever lived in the whole world."

Shasta then recites the long list of difficulties he has faced since leaving Bree and the others just a few hours earlier. Tears start to roll down his cheeks but suddenly are stopped by the knowledge that someone or some *thing* very large is walking beside him in the mist. Eventually the mysterious creature speaks and invites Shasta to tell him all his sorrows.

Reassured by the creature's deep, gentle voice and warm breath, Shasta looks back on a life filled with sorrow. He tells how he was brought up by a hard-hearted fisherman and never knew his real father or mother. Then during the escape they were chased by wild lions and forced to swim for their lives. The night alone at the tombs was terrifying as beasts howled at him from the desert. Then just as they were about to reach their goal, another lion seemed to come out of nowhere, chasing them and wounding Aravis. The creature explains to him,

> I do not call you unfortunate....I was the lion who forced you to join with Aravis. I was the cat who comforted you among the houses of the dead. I was the lion who drove the jackals from you while you slept. I was the lion who gave the horses the new strength of fear for the last mile so that you should reach King Lune in time. And I was the lion you do not remember who pushed the boat in which you lay, a child near death, so that it came to shore where a man sat, wakeful at midnight, to receive you.

All along, from the moment he was rescued by the fisherman to his current journey through the mountains in the fog, Shasta has been watched over and helped in ways he never knew. Rather than being the most unfortunate boy that ever lived, Shasta sees that he has been surrounded by a strange fortune all his life. As Shasta comes to realize, "It wasn't luck at all really, it was *Him*."

Bringing Narnia Home

In *Prince Caspian*, Peter, Susan, Edmund, and Lucy complete a long and dangerous journey before they finally arrive at the Narnians' camp. In the film version, Caspian and Peter come upon each other unexpectedly and, mistaking each other for enemies, begin to fight. Suddenly Peter sees the Narnian troops who have gathered around them. "Prince Caspian?" he asks, stepping back.

"Yes. And who are you?" Caspian demands, slowly lowering his sword.

The others run up, and Susan calls out, "Peter!"

"*High King* Peter?" Caspian asks, his voice filled with disbelief.

"I believe you called," Peter states, a reference to Susan's horn.

"Yes, but...." Caspian says haltingly, "I thought you'd be...older."

"Well if you like," Peter responds, "we can come back in a few years."

"No, it's all right!" says Caspian and then adds, "You're not exactly what I expected."

Caspian may perhaps be forgiven for not recognizing the help that has been sent to him, for it comes in a strange form and is not what *anyone* was expecting. And this is precisely Lewis's point. Sometimes help may not look like help, not until much later.

"Further In"

Questions for Reflection

1. Can you think of examples in other stories or fairytales where help does not look like help or

comes in an unexpected way? (For example, if you know the story of Beauty and the Beast, do you think being changed into a beast could be considered a form of strange help?)

2. Has help ever appeared in your own life in a way that may have not seemed like help? What did that involve?

3. Have you ever been surprised when you were unexpectedly able to help someone? What was that like?

CHAPTER 5

LIVE LIKE IT'S ALWAYS
CHRISTMAS AND NEVER WINTER

*Merriment and Celebration Are Not Just for
Holidays and Birthdays*

A WONDERFUL TEA

Readers who point to the scene early in *The Lion, the Witch and the Wardrobe* where Edmund eats a whole box of Turkish Delight and think Lewis is saying that *enjoying delicious things to eat is wrong* must be overlooking all the other scrumptious meals in the story.

Early on Mr. and Mrs. Beaver serve the four children one of the most famous dinners in all the Chronicles: good freshwater fish right out of the pond, boiled potatoes with butter (as much as you want), and a great and gloriously sticky marmalade roll for dessert. Following the four children's coronation at the end of the book, there is a great feast in Cair Paravel with revelry, dancing, and loads to eat and drink. And of course, on the very first trip that Lucy makes to Narnia, she is invited to have tea with Mr. Tumnus, where he serves hard-boiled eggs, sardines on toast, buttered toast, toast with honey, and a sugar-topped cake. As the narrator reports, "It was a wonderful tea."

So what *is* Lewis saying?

Lewis's point is that our attitude toward the pleasures God has made and toward all created things has two components: (1) we are to enjoy them, but (2) we are not supposed to idolize them or make them the most important things in our life. Or put another way, when it comes to pleasures, we are to go for *enjoyment,* not *enslavement.*

While most readers get Lewis's second point about not making pleasures into obsessions, they sometimes overlook his first one. At Lucy's tea with Mr. Tumnus, he complains that since the arrival of the White Witch in Narnia, it is *always winter and never Christmas.* Lewis's message to us is the exact opposite. Merriment is not just for holidays and birthdays—we should live like it's *always Christmas and never winter.*

NARNIA'S MERRY MAKERS

During Lucy's first visit with Mr. Tumnus, he describes what Narnia was like before the White Witch.

He tells her about the midnight dances in the forest with the spirits of the trees and about feasting and treasure-seeking with the dwarfs. He explains how in summer old Silenus would come to visit and sometimes even Bacchus himself would appear, and then the whole forest would be filled for weeks on end with what he refers to as *jollification*.

Mr. Tumnus's point is that when an evil tyrant is not forbidding it, Narnia is filled to the brim and overflowing with fun and merriment.

One of the first signs that the Witch's spell over Narnia is beginning to break is the arrival of Father Christmas. "She has kept me out for a long time," he explains to Peter, Susan, and Lucy, "but I have got in at last." After Father Christmas delivers his special gifts to each of the children, he reaches into his bag and pulls out a tray with cups and saucers, a bowl of sugar, a jug of cream, and finally a big teapot.

"Merry Christmas!" he cries as he climbs back into his sleigh and his reindeer pull away. And then Mr. Beaver cuts bread for sandwiches, Mrs. Beaver pours out the tea, and, as Lewis tells us, "Everyone enjoyed themselves."

Enjoying yourself is one thing that the White Witch seems to hate the most. At one point in the story, as she is making her way to the Stone Table with the dwarf driving her great sleigh and Edmund as her prisoner, they come upon a group of Narnian merrymakers who also have been visited by Father Christmas. There is holly, plum pudding, and something good to drink. As they sit together around a table in the woods, everyone is clearly having fun.

"What is the meaning of all this gluttony, this waste, this self-indulgence?" the Witch demands. When she discovers the festive elements were a gift from Father Christmas, she becomes even more enraged and commands the troop of merrymakers to say that he has not been there. When they refuse, they are turned into statues so they will never make merry again.

In the Gospels, Jesus says this about his intentions for those who follow him: "I came that they may have life, and have it abundantly" (John 10:10 NASB). Aslan would say the same. In fact, his visits to Narnia are made for that very reason, to ensure that his followers whose lives have been threatened might be freed from danger, and then that they do not merely survive but live more abundantly—more fully and with more enjoyment—than they did under their wicked oppressors.

The Witch's policy is the exact opposite of having life and having it more abundantly. As we have seen, not all of her subjects even get to live. Those who do live in a way that is anything but abundant. Under the White Witch's rule, abundance and enjoyment are nonexistent. When Edmund comes to the Witch's castle, he is served a hunk of dry bread and an iron bowl with some water in it. Under Aslan's rule, enjoyment takes place in extra-large amounts, and there is always plenty to go around. His whole reason for coming is to change a miserable Narnia back into a joyous Narnia, as Mr. Beaver explains: "Wrong will be right, when Aslan comes in sight."

It Was a Romp

When you were little, did you ever see a beautiful lion in the zoo and wish it somehow would be possible to play with it? Susan and Lucy have this wish come true in Narnia. The scene that takes place after Aslan returns to life in *The Lion, the Witch and the Wardrobe* is one of the most loved in all the Chronicles. In fact, when the book was first released, it was this scene that was chosen for the front cover.

The resurrected Aslan tells Susan and Lucy he can feel his strength returning. Then he cries, "Catch me if you can!" With eyes bright and tail flicking, Aslan leaps high over the girls' heads and lands on the other side. Around the hilltop where the Stone Table now lies in pieces, a mad chase begins with Aslan in the lead and Lucy and Susan close behind. One moment Aslan is hopelessly out of reach, the next he is almost close enough for them to catch his tail. One moment he is diving between them, the next he is tossing them into the air. Now he races ahead at full speed. Now he stops on a dime, and all three roll together in a laughing heap. Lewis reports, "It was such a romp as no one has ever had except in Narnia."

Of course the wildest romp in Narnia takes place near the end of *Prince Caspian*, when Silenus and Bacchus appear—just as Mr. Tumnus had told about during Lucy's tea. Within no time everyone is playing, laughing, and eating the grapes that seem to be growing everywhere.

"Is it a romp, Aslan?" asks Bacchus. And the narrator replies, "Apparently it was." Then there is more play, more laughter, more merriment, and more grape-eating until finally everyone flops down breathless on the ground.

Things get even merrier the next morning as Aslan wakes Susan and Lucy with the announcement: "We will make holiday." With flutes playing and cymbals clashing, the whole party sets off with Lucy and Susan riding on Aslan's back, followed by Bacchus and his wild girls, with Silenus and his donkey bringing up the rear. While Peter and Caspian are fighting Miraz's army, Aslan and his happy troop must undo the gloomy effects of the tyrant's harsh reign.

The holiday reaches the river bank, where Aslan

casts down the stone bridge, freeing the river once again. Splashing across what is now the Fords of Beruna, the revelers continue on to a school where a group of cramped, confined, and otherwise miserable students are let out of class. As the company continues on, freedom and merriment break out wherever they go. And so at last "with leaping and dancing and singing, with music and laughter and roaring and barking and neighing"—they arrive back at the place where Miraz's army is surrendering.

Lewis wants to remind us that celebration and merriment are not something just for birthdays and holidays. He also wants to say that—to the degree it is possible—they are not something just for good times, but for hard times as well. In Narnia we learn that there is a gladness that can underlie any sorrow, a type of joy that never leaves us.

We find this remarkable kind of joy in Prince Rilian at the end of *The Silver Chair*. While still trapped deep underground beneath the surface of Narnia, surrounded by presumed enemies, and with the floodwaters rising, the Prince leads the group as he, Jill, Eustace, and Puddleglum make their way toward higher ground. But rather than being filled with panic or despair, Rilian simply urges the others to remember that Aslan will always be their good lord, whether he means them to live or die.

The narrator describes the strange gladness that seems to fill the prince: "Unlike the other three, he seemed to be almost enjoying himself. He whistled as he rode and sang snatches of an old song."

BRINGING NARNIA HOME

In *The Last Battle*, Jill and Eustace experience a tranquil time in-between dangerous encounters. As Jill walks beside Jewel the Unicorn simply enjoying the warm spring afternoon, she exclaims, "Oh, this *is* nice! Just walking along like this." Then Jill expresses her wish that there could be more times when nothing much happens.

Jewel explains to Jill that because the children are brought out of their world only when Narnia is in danger, she must not think it is always like that. In-between these perilous times are whole centuries filled with good, ordinary times when there is hardly anything dramatic enough to record in the history books. Dances, feasts, and tournaments are the only notable things, and every day and week is better than the last.

The Chronicles of Narnia do not record all of Narnian history. In all those years that come between the children's visits, the Narnians do not go back to being miserable like they were under the White Witch or King Miraz. They celebrate each good day with good, ordinary merriment—and in doing so, they remind us that if we really want to live like a Narnian, we have to celebrate like one.

"FURTHER IN"

QUESTIONS FOR REFLECTION

1. Can you think of other great celebrations or feasts in the Narnia stories or other fairytales?

2. When some people look at Christians, they may see a joyless, disapproving group of people who never seem to have any fun. What might Lewis be saying to Christians today?

3. What about yourself—do you laugh as often as you should? What might you do to celebrate each ordinary day more?

CHAPTER 6

IT TAKES A VILLAGE TO MAKE A COMMUNITY

(With Giants, Dwarfs, and Everything In-Between)

TWO VERY DIFFERENT SORTS OF ARMIES

There are some books where the illustrations play as important a role as the words and come to be loved just as much. Such is the case for the illustrations found in *The Chronicles of Narnia*. Pauline Baynes was only in her twenties and just beginning her career when she first met C. S. Lewis and was invited to work on the project. Despite her lack of experience, Baynes was somehow able to capture the very essence of the enchanted world and its inhabitants through the pen-and-ink drawings she created. In fact, her illustrations have become such a big part of the stories that it is hard to imagine the books without them.

One of Baynes's most-revealing illustrations is found in chapter 14 of *Prince Caspian*, where Peter and Miraz fight in single combat.

"*It is our pleasure to adventure our royal person on behalf of our trusty and well-beloved Caspian in clean wager of battle....*" The letter sent by High King Peter to Miraz the Usurper challenges him—in proper courtly language—to a fight to the death or until one of them yields. And so on a warm summer's afternoon at the agreed-upon hour of two o'clock, the two forces gather around a square space of level grass (called the lists), which has been marked out between the two armies with ropes and stakes.

In Pauline Baynes's drawing we can see the six Marshals of the Lists in their respective places. Two Telmarines stand in the far corners, and one stands in the middle of the left side. At the Narnian corners are Giant Wimbleweather and the Bulgy Bear, who, despite being warned not to, is sucking his paws. Glenstorm the Centaur stands—motionless and noble, half man and half horse—in the middle on the right side. In the middle of the roped-off space, Peter and Miraz have just begun to fight.

The Telmarine forces watch from the far side of the lists, all the same height, all the same age, all dressed in the same battle gear, all looking exactly the same. In the foreground on this side of the combat, the Narnian troops also watch as the two leaders circle each other warily. But while the Telmarines all look virtually identical to one another, the Narnians all look different.

On the right, close to the rope, we can see Doctor Cornelius, who is half dwarf and half man; Prince Caspian, a Telmarine boy of about twelve; and King Edmund, an English boy a year or two younger. Standing behind Peter and Caspian and craning his neck to see over them is the faithful badger Trufflehunter. On the left side in back of Giant Wimbleweather (and looking quite small by comparison), we can see Trumpkin the dwarf waving his hands and cheering excitedly. In the middle are a fox, two rabbits, a beaver, another badger, a large mouse (presumably Reepicheep), a faun, another bear, a squirrel, an otter, a wolf, and a cat.

In Pauline Baynes's picture, we have a great illustration (literally) of Lewis's point that it takes all sorts of people—giants, dwarfs, and everything in between—to make a community.

Narnia would not be Narnia if it was all badgers.

The Dragon and the Mouse

In *The Voyage of the Dawn Treader,* one of the first things we learn about Eustace is that he has no friends. And yet, despite this fact, he is quite glad when he hears that his cousins Edmund and Lucy are coming for a visit—not because he will finally have some company but because, as Lewis tells us, deep inside he likes "bossing and bullying." And if you like this sort of thing, the first thing you are going to need is someone to bully and boss.

You might think that being sent through a magical painting out of your world and into another one, being plopped down into the middle of the ocean, and then boarding a ship where animals can talk might shake a person up. Might cause him to rethink his life a bit.

Not Eustace.

Within a few days, Eustace locates the smallest creature on the ship and, imagining he can torment him, comes up with a plan. We are told that Eustace thinks it would be "delightful" to catch hold of Reepicheep's long tail, to swing him around once or twice, and then to run away and laugh. This is the first action Eustace takes since arriving in Narnia, and here we see his central reason for living, the formula for the only version of happiness he knows: to dominate, torment, and intimidate others. This is what he was up to in Lucy's bedroom before he was interrupted by the picture of the sailing ship. Now he gets back to the real business of his life.

Despite being swung around by the tail,

Reepicheep—who has been in far worse situations—needs only a moment to draw his sword and jab Eustace's hand. Once he is let go, the noble mouse turns to face his former tormentor and demand the satisfaction of a duel.

Given this rocky start, the special friendship that develops between Eustace and Reepicheep is all the more touching and amazing.

After Eustace is transformed into a dragon, he comes to see how dragonish he has been. As Lewis comments, it is clear to everyone that Eustace's character was "rather improved" by becoming a dragon. Now rather than trying to avoid work, he is eager to help in any way he can. One of his first actions is to tear up and bring back a great pine tree to serve as a new mast for the *Dawn Treader*.

Although he enjoys the newfound pleasures of being liked and liking other people, Eustace shudders at his hideous reflection and is afraid to be alone with himself. At the same time, he is ashamed to be with the others. On rainy and chilly evenings, he is a comfort to the crew as everyone sits with their backs up against his hot sides. And on evenings when his heat is not needed, he slinks away. But here we find the unexpected turn as Lewis reports: "On such occasions, greatly to his surprise, Reepicheep was his most constant comforter."

And so begins one of the most delightful, albeit surprising, friendships in all of Narnia—the friendship between a great dragon and a great-hearted mouse.

On those nights when he sees that Eustace is absent, Reepicheep quietly slips away from the merry fellowship around the fire and goes off to find him. Then he sits by the giant head, always upwind to avoid the constant smoke, and recounts stories of countless heroes who, like Eustace, had fallen into distressing circumstances but had recovered and lived happily ever after.

Here again we find the illustration by Pauline Baynes perfectly captures the moment. Off in the distance we see the figures of the crew around the campfire, and beyond them we can make out the silhouette of the ship. In the foreground, surrounded by the inky night, the forlorn dragon is stretched out on the sand, comforted by a mouse who is clearly telling a lively tale.

Once more we find Lewis's message about community. Why should a dragon and a mouse be friends? On the surface they seem awfully different from each other. What could they possibly have in common?

As it turns out, what they have in common is something that is greater than their external differences. As we, along with Eustace (to his great astonishment), soon discover, he too has a great heart.

WHAT FATHER CHRISTMAS KNOWS

As we move on from the memorable image of the dragon and the mouse, we find Lewis's reminder that even when characters *do* look alike externally, real community is made up of individuals who have different gifts, different temperaments, and different abilities. Perhaps the best example of this principle is seen in the Pevensie children, siblings from the same family but each very different from the rest.

We see this difference in chapter 10 of *The Lion, the Witch and the Wardrobe*, when Father Christmas arrives in Narnia for the first time in many years. As he passes out gifts to Peter, Susan, and Lucy, he does not give them all the same thing. Instead he gives them presents especially suited to their unique abilities and inclinations and to the unique contribution each will be called to make. Peter is given a sword and a shield, Susan receives a bow and her magic horn, and Lucy is given her healing cordial and a small dagger.

Is Lewis saying here that males cannot be archers or healers? Not at all. In Narnia, as in all real communities, each person is recognized as an individual and is called upon to put his or her unique abilities and inclinations to use. If Peter is better suited to use a sword and shield in the service of Narnia, Lucy is better suited to serve as a healer, and, as we see in *Prince Caspian*, Susan is better suited to serve as an archer.

We might also note that Lucy is the youngest of the four children, and her youth also seems to be a factor in her role here as a healer. Lewis shows us a much older Lucy in *The Horse and His Boy*. And there he has her play a different role, as we see her riding into battle wearing a helmet and a mail shirt, carrying a bow and a quiver full of arrows.

In *The Horse and His Boy*, Lewis revisits his point about differences when he has Shasta explain that in times of war, "Everyone must do what he can do best." Or—given Lucy's new role, what *she* can do best. Lewis continues this theme in *The Last Battle* when Tirian, Eustace, and Jill must travel through dense thickets that make it hard to get a bearing. Jill is clearly the best pathfinder. And because of this, Tirian puts her in front to lead.

After receiving her dagger and being told it must be used only in self-defense, Lucy wants to know why Father Christmas does not want her in the battle, and her words show both humility and self-awareness. She tells him, "I think—I don't know—but I think I could be brave enough."

Father Christmas does not question Lucy's bravery, nor do we. In fact, near the end of the story Lewis makes it clear that Lucy is brave enough by having her become known as "Lucy the Valiant" during her reign as a queen of Narnia. In giving Lucy this title,

Lewis sends a message that courage is not limited to the battlefield, nor is it limited to one specific kind of contribution. He also sends the message that real community is made up of different kinds of individuals, each with a unique part to play.

BRINGING NARNIA HOME

One of the best depictions of the diversity we find in Narnia occurs in *The Lion, the Witch and the Wardrobe* when Aslan breathes on the marble-like statues in the Witch's castle and brings them back to life in a variety of hues from all across the spectrum. We are told,

> Instead of all that deadly white the courtyard was now a blaze of colors; glossy chestnut sides of centaurs, indigo horns of unicorns, dazzling plumage of birds, reddy-brown of foxes, dogs, and satyrs, yellow stockings and crimson hoods of dwarfs; and the birch-girls in silver, and the beech-girls in fresh, transparent green, and the larch-girls in green so bright that it was almost yellow.

In the final chapter of *The Last Battle*, Lewis further expands his notion of community. As Lucy looks out from the garden in Aslan's Country, she can see other countries like spurs jutting out from a great mountain range. Narnia is just one spur. The country of Calormen is on another spur, and England is on yet another. If it's true that Narnia would not be Narnia if it was all badgers, we can also say that Aslan's Country would not be Aslan's Country if it was all Narnia.

"FURTHER IN"

QUESTIONS FOR REFLECTION

1. From Bacchus to beavers, from centaurs to sea people, Lewis seems to delight in differences. How many *different* kinds of characters can you list from the seven Narnia books?

2. Besides the great friendship that develops between Eustace and Reepicheep, we also have the special friendship between Lucy and Mr. Tumnus. Think about some of your own friends. What are some of the differences you've noted between you and each of them? In what ways do the differences make your friendship deeper or stronger?

3. Can you come up with something you like that could be classified as different? What makes *you* one of a kind?

CHAPTER 7

THERE IS A WAY BACK FROM EVERY OFFENSE— LARGE AND SMALL

(And It Has Nothing to Do with Having a Good Defense)

LUCY SPIES ON A FRIEND

Halfway through *The Voyage of the Dawn Treader*, the crew drops anchor at a mysterious island they later learn is called the Island of the Voices. Immediately a landing party is sent ashore to search for food and water. Not realizing the island is inhabited by a fierce race of invisible people, the group on land soon is cut off from the ship by a crowd of the unseen combatants and presented with a strange demand.

"We want something that little girl can do for us," the Chief Voice says, indicating Lucy, and then goes on to tell a long, drawn-out tale. The Chief explains that he and his countrymen were servants of the great magician who owns the island. One day the magician gave them an order they refused to obey. To punish them for their disobedience, the magician put them under an "uglifying" spell. Seeking to undo their uglification, they crept into the magician's great house by night and made their way upstairs to the room where his magic book was located. Unable to find a spell that would change them back, they settled on one that made them all invisible.

The long and short of it is, the Chief concludes, they now have become "mortal tired of being invisible" and need a little girl to go back upstairs to the magic book to find and say the spell that will take off their invisibleness—for the spell will not work unless it is said by a little girl or by the magician himself. Should Lucy refuse, the Chief threatens to cut their throats.

Lucy agrees to their demand and soon finds herself saying an anxious goodbye to the others and mounting the stairs. After passing a number of frightening obstacles, she finally arrives at the proper room and locates the magician's book. And what a book it is!

As Lucy turns the pages, she comes across cures for warts, toothache, and cramps. There are instructions on how to find buried treasure, how to remember things you have forgotten, and how to forget things you do not want to remember. There are words that can be used to call up or to prevent wind, fog, snow, sleet, or rain, and a magical way to tell if someone is telling the truth. Every page is illustrated with pictures so real they almost seem alive, and each spell is so fascinating Lucy finds it hard to tear herself away to look for the spell that reverses invisibility, which she was sent to find.

Soon she comes to a page with a spell promising to make the person who says it beautiful "beyond the lot of mortals." Always feeling overshadowed by her sister Susan's good looks, Lucy is about to say the spell when suddenly Aslan's face appears on the page. He is growling and has such an angry look on his face that Lucy turns the page at once. A short time later, she comes to a spell that can be used to let you know what your friends think about you. Though she senses it is wrong to do so, Lucy gives in to temptation and says the spell—partly, she tells herself, to make up for not being able to try the beautifying spell.

Gradually a picture of two schoolgirls sitting in an English train appears on the page. One is Lucy's friend, Marjorie Preston. The other is the school snob, Anne Featherstone. Lucy listens in as Anne makes cutting remarks about her, and to Lucy's horror, she hears Marjorie go along with them. "Not a bad little kid in her way," Marjorie concludes, "but I was getting pretty tired of her."

Calling the Marjorie in the picture a "two-faced

little beast," Lucy decides their friendship is over. Eventually she finds the spell that promises "to make *hidden* things visible," and, to her surprise, after she says the spell, Aslan appears in the room—where, he tells her, he has been all along. Something else that has been hidden also is made visible—Aslan brings up the fact that Lucy has been eavesdropping on her two classmates. Lucy offers a feeble excuse, suggesting that her listening in on a private conversation was not really eavesdropping since it was done by magic.

"Spying on people by magic is the same as spying on them in any other way," admonishes Aslan.

Here Lewis pauses in a story filled with suspense and high adventure to comment on a minor wrongdoing many people would overlook—but not Aslan. Lucy has spied on her friend, Aslan points it out to her, and Lucy comes to see her mistake.

"Oh dear," she worries. "Have I spoiled everything?"

Aslan does not say Lucy will be able to forget the hurtful words she has heard, but he tells her she has misjudged her friend. "She is weak, but she loves you," Aslan assures her and then explains that Marjorie's fear caused her to say things she did not mean.

Lucy responds with two simple words that make up the formula for the way back from all the offenses in Narnia—great and small. Said with sincerity and genuine repentance without becoming defensive or making excuses, these words have a magic of their own to make any wrong right again.

"I'm sorry," Lucy says.

IT'S MY FAULT

There is a kind of book where the protagonists are very nearly perfect. They never seem to be tempted by the sorts of things readers are tempted by. They never snap at their friends or siblings. They never quarrel, become irritable, or even complain very much despite the fact that the ordeals they face are incredibly demanding and the conditions they endure are extremely unpleasant. They never seem to make the sort of mistakes we ourselves make. If they break the rules or do something wrong, it is always in the service of some greater good. And so, in this type of book, we can go from start to finish without ever finding an apology.

This is not the kind of book that Lewis wants to write. *The Chronicles of Narnia* are full of mistakes, big and small, though as we have seen, Lewis does not really want to label any moral failing as small. And because they are full of mistakes, the Narnia stories are also full of characters who need to say they are sorry. Perhaps no story more so than *The Silver Chair*.

"There is no denying," the narrator begins chapter 7, "it was a beast of a day." As Jill, Eustace, and

Puddleglum trudge beneath a sunless sky, the gray clouds are heavy with the potential for snow. Beneath their feet, the ground is frozen hard. Blowing over the frozen ground is a wind that we are told feels "as if it would take your skin off." Soon the threat of snow gives way to a fierce snowstorm, one that shows no sign of letting up and drives the thick flakes into their faces so hard they can barely see.

This is not the first beastly day the travelers have had on their quest. So besides being cold, they are also weary and hungry. Soon the ancient road they have been following becomes much more ruinous, forcing them to scramble over great broken stones and rubble. "Hard going for sore feet," the narrator reports, but too cold to stop for a rest.

So perhaps what happens next is not so surprising. When Puddleglum, the faithful Marsh-wiggle who has been their companion on the journey, asks Jill if she is sure of the signs Aslan gave her to remember and wants to know which one they are supposed to be watching for, she snaps at him.

"Oh, come *on*! Bother the signs," she cries in annoyance.

Eustace, who has already been on a previous adventure to Narnia and should know better, does not come to Puddleglum's aid, but makes the same mistake as Jill.

"For goodness' sake," Eustace complains, "let's get on."

In *The Voyage of the Dawn Treader*, when Lucy listened in on the private conversation between Marjorie Preston and Anne Featherstone, she knew in her heart it was wrong, but it was not as though she had been previously cautioned about this offense in the story. Here in *The Silver Chair*, we might say that Jill's transgression is worse, for at the start of the story she was specifically warned that the signs would not look at all like she expected them to. Because of this, Aslan told Jill to say them to herself when she woke each morning and when she went to bed each night. "Let nothing turn your mind from following the signs," Aslan had commanded.

Of all the British children who travel to Narnia, Jill seems to be one of the hardiest and least in need of some great change in her character or attitude. So how do we get from Aslan's command to Jill's outburst? How do we get from *Let nothing turn your mind from following the signs* to *Bother the signs*?

While never excusing his characters' mistakes, Lewis always helps us to understand them and so to feel compassion for characters who are less than perfect and thus more like us. Besides the snow, cold, hunger, and weariness, Jill is thinking of the hot baths, soft beds, and scrumptious meals they were promised if they could reach the castle of Harfang before the gates are shut.

All at once, high on the plain above them, the lights of the castle appear. When Puddleglum once more tries to bring their focus back to the quest, Jill snaps again—this time worse than the time before.

"Oh, shut up," she tells the well-meaning Marsh-wiggle. "We haven't a moment to lose."

In a different kind of book, remarks like this might be overlooked. In other books, things far worse than this are said and ignored. Not in the Narnia stories. Jill has committed a rather serious offense, one that she will need to apologize for and does—though not right away.

The next morning, the travelers—now warm, bathed, well-rested, and well-fed—look out from one the castle's high windows. Suddenly they realize that the ruins they were scrambling in the day before have the words UNDER ME carved deep into the pavement. They instantly recognize it as one of the signs Aslan told them they were to watch for.

"It's my fault," Jill immediately says, and it is significant that she does not add any excuse about being cold, tired, or hungry. When Puddleglum tries to take some of the blame, claiming that he did not try hard enough to make the children stop, Eustace tells him, "You're the only one who isn't to blame."

When Eustace declares that they simply must own up to the fact that of the four signs, they have "muffed the first three," Jill jumps in to say, "You mean I have."

"It's quite true," she continues. Then looking back on all the mistakes she has made since arriving in Narnia—including being responsible for Eustace's falling off the cliff at the start of their adventure—she confesses, "I've spoiled everything ever since you brought me here."

I've spoiled everything. While *everything* may be a bit of an overstatement, Jill *has* made a number of mistakes, ones that have caused them a great deal of hardship, and here she accepts the blame for the harm she has done. And then comes the magic, just as it did with Lucy's offense of spying on her friend. Turning to Puddleglum and Eustace, Jill says to them, "I'm frightfully sorry." And as before, with these words wrong is made right.

Lewis wants readers to see that there is a way back from every offense—great and small. And that way is through a heartfelt apology. For Lewis, this is needed, and this is *all* that is needed. Properly said, the apology does not need to be repeated over and over—that's how the magic works—although these words may need to be said again to others. When Jill meets Aslan at the end of *The Silver Chair*, she remembers how she made Eustace fall over the cliff and how she muffed nearly all the signs. She thinks back on all her snappings and quarrelings. And then Jill wants to say the same two miraculous words to Aslan: *I'm sorry*.

EDMUND'S BETRAYAL

Lewis wants readers to believe there is a way back from every offense, not just those we might view as relatively minor ones, such as spying on your friends or snapping at someone. In order to do this, he needs to show us a character who has done about the worst thing a person can do, who then is reunited with those he has wronged. And this is exactly what Lewis does in *The Lion, the Witch and the Wardrobe*.

"You have a traitor there, Aslan," says the White Witch during the visit she makes to Aslan's camp under promise of safe conduct. She declares that according to the Deep Magic, every traitor belongs to her and for every treachery she has a right to a kill.

The traitor she is referring to is, of course, Edmund. His treachery was to betray Peter, Susan, and Lucy—his own brother and sisters. It does not come much worse than this. Edmund will admit as much in *The Voyage of the Dawn Treader*, where he tells Eustace, "You haven't been as bad as I was on my first trip to Narnia. You were only an ass, but I was a traitor."

But by the time the White Witch arrives at the camp to claim what belongs to her, things have already been made right between Edmund and his siblings. After a very special talk with Aslan, one that no one else heard and Edmund never forgot, Aslan had presented Edmund to the very ones he had betrayed with these words: "Here is your brother, and—there is no need to talk to him about what is past."

There is no need for Peter, Susan, or Lucy to talk to Edmund about what is past. But there is a need for *Edmund* to say something about the past, a critical need. Without saying what he says next, there is no authentic way back from his offense—just a sweeping under the rug. In just eighteen words, Lewis shows us the way that wrong can be made right as readers are told, "Edmund shook hands with each of the others and said to each of them in turn, 'I'm sorry.'"

I'm sorry. Without these words, Edmund remains Edmund the traitor. With them, he admits he was wrong, makes it clear he regrets what he did, and once again becomes Edmund their brother. *I'm sorry*. With this short phrase, Edmund leaves the Witch's side and joins Aslan's side, the right side, the side where Edmund the traitor will become Edmund the Just, a king of Narnia. *I'm sorry*. With these words, Lewis shows us there is a way back from even the very worst offense. And it all starts with these words.

I'm sorry.

In the Gospels we find the story of Judas, who

betrays Jesus and then goes off and hangs himself. We also find the story of Peter, who denies Christ and then goes off and weeps bitter tears of repentance. Peter realized something that Judas never understood, and it is the same lesson Lewis has for us here, one we need to be reminded of again and again. What Peter discovered is that there is always a way back—even from the very worst offense.

Bringing Narnia Home

We have seen in the Chronicles that both Edmund and Lucy make mistakes and must say, "I'm sorry." What about Peter and Susan? Lewis has the future High King of Narnia set a good example by having him make the very first apology in *The Lion, the Witch and the Wardrobe*. Because Peter had doubted Lucy's story about traveling through the wardrobe to Narnia and had even gone with Susan to see the Professor about her, the moment Peter realizes they are in a different land, he turns at once to Lucy and makes a sincere apology for not having believed her. Peter first says, "I apologize," then adds, "I'm sorry," and finally he asks if Lucy will shake hands.

Later in the story, Peter has a second apology to make. When they finally reach the Stone Table, Aslan asks where Edmund is. Mr. Beaver explains that Edmund has betrayed them and has joined the White

Witch. Then we are told that something—presumably his conscience—makes Peter say, "That was partly my fault, Aslan. I was angry with him and I think that helped him to go wrong."

In *Prince Caspian* we find that Susan must apologize to Lucy for not believing her about seeing Aslan on the riverbank and telling them to follow. "I see him now," Susan will tell her younger sister and then simply adds, "I'm sorry." And this is enough.

Once we start looking for them, we discover that *The Chronicles of Narnia* are full of apologies. After Aslan changes him back into a boy, Eustace makes a particularly heartfelt apology for having been so beastly. After Aravis has her meeting with the great lion at the end of *The Horse and His Boy*, the first thing she tells Cor is "There's something I've got to say at once. I'm sorry I've been such a pig."

What these apologies have in common is that they are genuine. We all have been offered a false apology, words that may sound like an apology but are a long way from being one. People making false apologies often use phrases such as *I'm sorry, but…* or *I'm sorry if…* Edmund makes a pretty good one of these after he follows Lucy through the wardrobe and discovers that her story, which earlier he had made fun of, is really true.

"I'll say I'm sorry if you like," he tells her. Lewis

makes it clear that *I'll say I'm sorry if you like* will not do. Nor will any statement that takes the general form of *I'm sorry if you were offended by my actions* or *I'm sorry if something I did upset you*. Any apology that starts out *I'm sorry, but…* is also unacceptable. What is required is just *I'm sorry*—with no *if*s or *but*s.

"Further In"

Questions for Reflection

1. Readers might remember that one of Edmund's early defining characteristics was that "he did not like to admit that he had been wrong." This is a quality so many—perhaps even all of us—share. Why do you think it is so difficult for us to admit when we are wrong and say "I'm sorry"?

2. Lewis suggests there is a big difference between someone who does something wrong and apologizes and someone who does something wrong and never apologizes. Do you agree? Can you think of times in your own life you faced one or both of these situations when someone did something wrong to you? What were the circumstances? What were the feelings that resulted?

3. Can you remember a time when you had to say "I'm sorry"? Is there someone you still need to say these words to?

CHAPTER 8

BURY THE HATCHET AND DON'T PUT A MARKER ON THE SITE

Forgiveness Means Forgiving and *Forgetting*

A WOULD-BE KIDNAPPER IS FORGIVEN

We have looked at a number of examples from *The Chronicles of Narnia* where C. S. Lewis shows us characters who have done something wrong and want to say they are sorry. But what about the people they have wronged? How are they supposed to respond when someone has hurt them, snapped at them, failed to believe them, or even betrayed them, and then wants to apologize and be forgiven?

Lewis's answer is a simple one we see repeated again and again.

When anyone makes a genuine apology in Narnia, they are forgiven. Always. No matter what. They are forgiven *immediately*, not at some unspecified time in the future after the people they have wronged have had time to cool off and decide whether to forgive them or not. And they are forgiven *fully*, not grudgingly, not reluctantly, not partially, or as a mere formality. Genuine apologies are always followed by genuine forgiveness in Narnia. And for Lewis, this is the way it is supposed to work in our world as well. Learning this lesson is one of the reasons we are brought to Narnia, so that when we return home, we will take this practice of forgiveness with us and follow it in our own lives.

We are not even to the end of the second chapter of *The Lion, the Witch and the Wardrobe* before someone has done something wrong, quite wrong as it turns out, and apologizes and wants to be forgiven. We are as shocked as Lucy to discover that Mr. Tumnus—the friendly faun she met at the Lamp-post, who invited her for tea—has only pretended to be her friend so he could lull her to sleep with his enchanted flute and turn her over to the White Witch.

In the end, Mr. Tumnus is unable to go through with his wicked plans, even though he knows that if the Witch finds out he has disobeyed her orders, he will be turned to stone and added to her statue collection. Through his tears, the contrite faun confesses everything to Lucy, and then swiftly and stealthily escorts her back through the woods. Finally they reach the Lamp-post where, off in the distance between the trees, Lucy can see the back of the wardrobe leading to the Professor's spare room.

"Be off home as quick as you can," Mr. Tumnus says to Lucy, of whom he already has become very fond. "And—c-can you ever forgive me for what I meant to do?" he adds, knowing that if he is never to see her again, he needs to know that he has been forgiven.

Despite her fears, despite the danger, despite the shock she received when she learned Mr. Tumnus was in the pay of the White Witch, Lucy responds in a way that will be typical of her—with faith, courage, generosity, hope, and love. "Why, of course I can," Lucy tells the tormented faun, "shaking him heartily by the hand" to make it clear she really means it.

The next time Lucy sees her new friend, Mr. Tumnus is a stone statue standing in a long, gloomy hall at the Witch's castle. "Oh, do come quick," she says to Aslan. A moment later, Mr. Tumnus has been brought back to life, and he and Lucy are holding hands and "dancing round and round" with joy. His earlier plans of kidnapping her not only are fully forgiven, they are fully forgotten and never mentioned again.

A TRAITOR'S APOLOGY IS ACCEPTED

Mr. Tumnus did not actually betray Lucy. He had planned to, but he stopped. Edmund, on the other hand, really does betray his brother and sisters.

"They're in the little house on top of the dam just up with river—with Mr. and Mrs. Beaver," he tells the White Witch. And so we might think that forgiving Edmund will be harder. It isn't—despite the fact that Edmund's transgression has far greater consequences.

After Aslan had a private talk with him and presented Edmund to the others, Edmund shook hands with each one in turn and said, "I'm sorry." And at this point we can imagine all sorts of things we might have said if we had been the ones betrayed. *You'd better be sorry! How could you have done that to us? What were you thinking? After all we have done for you!* We might not have accepted Edmund's apology. And even if we did, we still might have brought up his offense again and again. But Aslan has told the others, "There is no need to talk to him about what is past." And since there is no need to bring up the past, they never do. What happens after Edmund's apology takes Lewis only six words to describe. We simply are told: "And everyone said, 'That's all right.'"

And all *is* right. Earlier we looked at what real apologies look like. Here Lewis shows us what true forgiveness looks like. We could say that although Edmund's offense was like scarlet, he is now made as white as snow. The wrong that he committed against the others is completely forgotten and gone, as far away as the east is from the west.

There is a scene in the story of Edmund's forgiveness that might have been nice for Lewis to have included in the final chapter of *The Lion, the Witch and the Wardrobe*. It might have been nice to have witnessed Edmund's apology to Mr. Tumnus for his role in the faun's arrest and subsequent punishment. But Lewis leaves that encounter to our imaginations—as he does Lucy's encounter with Marjorie Preston, later, back in England. He does include a scene in *The Horse and His Boy* where King Edmund and Mr. Tumnus are together in Tashbaan. There, Lewis makes it clear that the two are fully reconciled, as they are not only friends, but Edmund is also gladly sharing leadership responsibilities with the faun he earlier had wronged.

Lewis uses the story of Edmund's transgression and restoration to explore one further issue: the question of whether someone always needs to know the full extent of the harm they have caused. After Aslan's sacrifice and resurrection in *The Lion, the Witch and the Wardrobe*, Lucy and Susan have a brief debate about this complex topic. Lucy wonders if someone should tell Edmund that Aslan agreed to give his life in exchange for Edmund's. Susan is against telling him, claiming that "it would be too awful for him." She asks Lucy how she would feel if she were in Edmund's place.

"All the same I think he ought to know," Lucy states.

Lewis never makes it clear exactly what Edmund is told about the sacrifice Aslan made for him. We are told that he grows up to be a grave and quiet man, perhaps because he has learned about the serious consequences his wicked actions had. In *The Voyage of the Dawn Treader*, Edmund wants to explain to Eustace who Aslan is and tells him, "He is the great Lion, the son of the Emperor-beyond-the-Sea, who saved me and saved Narnia."

Who saved me and saved Narnia. Clearly by this time—in a way we never find out—Edmund has learned how Aslan died in his place.

After someone has apologized and been forgiven, do they always need to know the full extent of the harm they have caused? Lewis leaves this question somewhat open but seems to lean toward a *yes*, but only on three conditions. First, the person need not be told right away. Some time may need to pass before they can bear to know the total amount of harm they have done. The person may need to become stronger and more mature. Second, telling someone the whole truth about their offense can never be part of an attempt to make them feel worse. Third and finally, forgiveness does not depend on a full awareness of all the damage that has been caused. Forgiveness depends upon only one thing: being sorry and asking for forgiveness.

Aslan Shows How We Are to Forgive

Easy to say, hard to do: Whether it's a long-term goal, some change we want to make, or a task we have put off, we all have something that fits this description. Forgiving someone who has hurt us is certainly another of those things that can be easy to say, hard to do—and no wonder. When someone has wronged us, why *should* we forgive them? We haven't done anything wrong. We're not the ones who messed up. Why should *we* have to do anything? In *Mere Christianity*, C. S. Lewis puts it this way: "Everyone says forgiveness is a lovely idea, until they have something to forgive."

Easy to say, hard to do.

In *The Chronicles of Narnia*, Lewis offers two ways that make forgiveness less difficult. First, he makes it clear that everybody—including characters such as Peter and Lucy, who may seem nearly perfect to us—has something they need to be forgiven for. Here Lewis is drawing on the principle from the Lord's Prayer: *Forgive us our trespasses, as we forgive those who trespass against us.* If we are going to want to be forgiven ourselves, and we will, then we need to forgive others. In an essay entitled "On Forgiveness," Lewis puts it this way: "To be a Christian means to forgive the inexcusable because God has forgiven the inexcusable in you."

Second, Lewis includes scenes where Aslan forgives someone, and in doing so gives us a model of what real forgiveness looks like—especially in *Prince Caspian*.

Most readers find *Prince Caspian* to be a more serious book than *The Lion, the Witch and the Wardrobe*. On this second adventure, Peter, Susan, Edmund, and Lucy are older. Narnia is less black and white. And people are not always what they seem. Caspian discovers his uncle is not the loving Lord Protector he has pretended to be. Trumpkin learns that the four Pevensies are not the helpless children he initially assumed they were—not by a longshot. At the start of *Prince Caspian*, when the four Pevensies are whisked off the train platform in England and appear in Narnia, Narnia is so unrecognizable they are not even sure where they are.

Perhaps the biggest difference on this second adventure is that when Aslan appears alongside the gorge of the Rush River, only Lucy can see him. This was not the way Aslan had acted on the first adventure, when everyone could see him. And, as readers discover, this difference leads to a fair bit of quarreling and several big mistakes. Peter—who should have learned something on the first adventure about believing Lucy, no matter how strange her claim—disbelieves his younger sister again and casts the deciding vote to go *down* the river, not *up*, where, according to Lucy, Aslan wants them to go. And Lucy—who of all the characters has seemed most ready to follow Aslan whatever the circumstances—travels downstream with them.

The company has a long, difficult day following the Rush River down to the Fords of Beruna, where they are surprised by sentries, and forced to turn back and completely retrace their steps. After supper that evening, thoroughly exhausted, they all quickly fall asleep. But late in the night Lucy wakes "with the feeling that the voice she liked best in the world is calling her name." Following the voice deep into the woods, Lucy finally sees Aslan standing in the moonlight and rushes to him as if her heart would burst. Finally reaching the great Lion, she puts her arms around his neck and buries her face in his mane.

"Aslan. Dear Aslan," Lucy repeats over and over through her tears of joy. After a while, Aslan tells her they must be getting on their way, for Lucy has work to do and much time has been lost.

"Wasn't it a shame?" Lucy replies and begins to talk about how the others were to blame since they did not believe her. "From somewhere deep inside Aslan's body," the narrator tells us, "there came the faintest suggestion of a growl," and gradually Lucy comes to see that whether the others believed Aslan was there or not, she was still supposed to follow him. Aslan concludes by telling Lucy that she must go back and wake the others and tell them they must go with her immediately. As before on the riverbank, they will not be able to see Aslan, at least not at first. If they refuse to follow, she must go on alone.

Once again Lucy buries her head in Aslan's mane. But soon she sees how she was wrong for not having followed Aslan from the start and sees that the wasted day was her fault as well.

"I'm sorry, Aslan," she says. "I'm ready now."

And then Aslan focuses, not on the past and the mistake she made, but on the present and the future. "Now you are a lioness," he tells her. "Now all Narnia will be renewed."

Aslan's response to Peter after hearing his regrets about how everything he has done has gone wrong is similar. When Peter finally meets Aslan in chapter 11, the young High King exclaims, "I'm so sorry. I've been leading them wrong ever since we started."

Aslan simply says, "My dear son." And this is all he needs to say.

Now you are a lioness. My dear son. This, Lewis would say, is what true forgiveness looks like. We find this same forgetting-what-is-past in the parable of the prodigal son. After the wayward son confesses his error, he expects to be treated like a hired servant. Instead his father not only immediately welcomes him back but also calls for a feast to celebrate his return.

BRINGING NARNIA HOME

So far we have been looking at examples of forgiving characters who have felt sorry and apologized. The issue of forgiving people who express no remorse for their wickedness is a topic Lewis says little about except for one brief statement Prince Caspian makes after the evil dwarf Nikabrik is killed during the attempt to call up the White Witch.

"I am sorry for Nikabrik," the young prince says, though he admits that the dwarf hated him from the moment they met. Caspian then tells the others that the long years of suffering and hating had caused the dwarf to go "sour inside." "If we had won quickly he might have become a good Dwarf in the days of peace," Caspian concludes.

Nikabrik is dead, but it seems unlikely that if he had lived, he would have shown much, if any, contrition for his actions. And yet here in Caspian's tone, Lewis suggests there is something gracious and noble about extending forgiveness even to those who have not asked for it.

"FURTHER IN"

QUESTIONS FOR REFLECTION

1. In the essay "On Forgiveness" mentioned earlier, Lewis writes: "It is perhaps not so hard to forgive

a single great injury. But to forgive the incessant provocations of daily life—to keep on forgiving the bossy mother-in-law, the bullying husband, the nagging wife, the selfish daughter, the deceitful son—how can we do it?" In *The Chronicles of Narnia* we have the example of Edmund, who is forgiven for a single great injury, and the example of Eustace, who must be forgiven for a lifetime of incessant minor provocations before undergoing his great change. Which character would it be harder for you to forgive and why?

2. Aslan tells Edmund's siblings, "There is no need to talk to him about what is past." But he never tells *Edmund* not to bring up what is past. And at one point Edmund does—using his past errors to help comfort and reassure Eustace. Can you think of a negative way and a positive way we might remember our past sins? Describe the details.

3. The scene in *Prince Caspian* where Lucy finally meets Aslan and tells him she is sorry for not obeying him earlier and he concludes by telling her, "Now you are a lioness," is one of the most-beloved scenes in the Narnia stories. Can you think of a time when you have accepted someone's apology in a similar way, with encouragement instead of reproach?

CHAPTER 9

ONLY THE GOOD HAVE FUN

The Self-Centered Life Turns Out to Be Not Cool

ALWAYS WINTER AND NEVER CHRISTMAS

Long before the current glut of reality shows designed to give us ordinary folks an inside look at the lifestyle of some rich and famous celebrity or celebrity family, there was a show actually called *Lifestyles of the Rich and Famous*. Each week the dapper host would take us past the gates guarding their opulent residences and provide an up-close, behind-closed-doors peek at their supposedly glamorous lifestyles.

First, we would see the expansive grounds and perfectly manicured lawn and gardens. Then would come the garage with not one or two but a fleet of very fancy, very expensive cars. Moving on to the interior of the house, there would be a massive kitchen with multiple high-end stoves and ovens, a walk-in

86

refrigerator, and loads of counter space. At some point we would go out back to see the beautiful swimming pool and veranda. Back inside we would find drawer after drawer, closet after closet, filled with neatly arranged clothes, shoes, watches, and jewelry—all with expensive labels clearly displayed. Our last stop would be the giant bedroom with the oversized bed and its oversized pillows, presumably for the oversized heads of the people who lived there.

And all along, the implication of the snooty host is that if only we too could have all these things—the cars, the house, the pool, the stuff—then our lives would be so great, so much better than they are now.

In *The Lion, the Witch and the Wardrobe*, Lewis provides a similar behind-the-scenes look into the life of the rich and famous—in this case, the White Witch. But what he reveals is quite different from what we see in the so-called reality shows.

In chapter 9, when Edmund arrives at the Witch's castle, he must work his way past the crowd of statues in the courtyard, creatures who have been turned into stone for disobeying her orders. At one point he sees a little faun with a very sad expression on its face—the statue of Lucy's friend Mr. Tumnus. This is the Witch's warped idea of collecting original art. When Edmund goes inside, he enters a long, gloomy hall. At the far end is a single lamp giving off a weak light. Sitting next to this single lamp—all by herself and doing nothing—is the White Witch. The film version of the story expands on Lewis's description as moviegoers see a giant ice throne in the great hall, but nothing else.

During the hundred years of winter she has imposed over Narnia, what does the White Witch do all day? What does she do with all her power and wealth?

Nothing that could be called fun, interesting, or remotely glamorous.

Here is a look at the Witch's daily to-do list: (1) sharpen Stone Knife, (2) check statues, (3) sit on throne, (4) polish wand, (5) make sure it's still winter but never Christmas, (6) yell at wolves, and (7) check whether anyone is happy or enjoying themselves in any way—if so, torment or tyrannize them until they are not.

Even more revealing is what is *not* on the Witch's list. We do not see anything like (1) have fun, (2) hang out with friends, or (3) tell a joke and laugh. We could say that it's always winter and never Christmas not just in Narnia but also in the White Witch's heart.

Lewis provides a similar insight in his depiction of King Miraz from *Prince Caspian*, whose life of self-centeredness has led not to happiness and contentment but to misery and isolation. In the end, he is killed not in single combat with Peter, which might at least have been a noble death, but stabbed in the back by one of his own trusted advisors. It turns out that—contrary to what we were led to believe on *Lifestyles of the Rich and Famous*—the self-centered life is not cool or fun.

It is not even all that interesting.

A Most Disappointing Time

Of the four Pevensies, Edmund seems to smile the least. We are told that during his reign as king he is graver and quieter than the rest and is great in council and judgment. Because of this, he comes to be known as Edmund the Just. But if Edmund is grave and quiet, after his talk with Aslan he also has a deep-seated peace that never leaves him. Despite any chaos or confusion the four siblings encounter, Edmund always seems to have a quiet, unspoken joy running beneath his serene exterior.

But it was not always this way. For much of *The Lion, the Witch and the Wardrobe*, Edmund was miserable, really miserable, as he traveled down the same path of selfishness and self-deception that the White Witch and Miraz took.

In chapter 9 of *The Lion, the Witch and the Wardrobe*, Edmund slips away from the lovely dinner at the Beavers' and sets out on his own for the castle of the White Witch. While the others are safe, snug, and warm, Edmund is the very opposite.

The light is starting to fade and the snow is falling harder as Edmund crosses back over Mr. Beaver's dam. And with each step he takes into a life of selfishness and betrayal, conditions get worse. In the wintry darkness, he trudges through unseen snow drifts, falls over hidden tree trunks, and slides down steep banks, battering his shins until he is wet, cold, and bruised all over. And the conditions inside Edmund are even worse. As Lewis points out, "The silence and the loneliness were dreadful."

Once he arrives at the castle, Edmund soon discovers that the promises of the White Witch are all lies and the self-centered life is not going to be anything like he thought it would be. It turns out that only one person at a time can have it their way, and it's not going to be Edmund. The narrator sums up his whole experience in nine words, telling us: "Edmund meanwhile had been having a most disappointing time."

The key word here is *disappointing*. In a similar way, viewers raised on a steady diet of *Lifestyles of the Rich and Famous* are assured of being disappointed when they find that the happiness supposed to be theirs when they finally get that big house or fancy car or those expensive clothes is all an illusion.

Lewis's point is that the self-centered life makes a lot of promises but never delivers.

Learning that Peter, Susan, and Lucy are on their way to meet Aslan at the Stone Table, the Witch orders her sleigh to be made ready. Soon Edmund is racing with her through the night, covered with snow and wet to the bone. "And oh, how miserable he was!" Lewis reports as Edmund finally and fully realizes that the self-centered life is not at all anything like cool or fun.

PLEASED WITH NOTHING

Edmund lives the self-centered life for only a short while, and so it does not take him very long to see the truth about where this path is leading. This is not the case for his cousin Eustace.

When we meet Eustace at the start of *The Voyage of the Dawn Treader*, he has been on the self-centered path for so long that he cannot conceive of any other way to be. He does not see that he is self-centered. Nor does he realize that he is unhappy and miserable. Had the magical picture not taken him to Narnia when it did, he might have remained on this path for the rest of his life.

Earlier we looked at the To-Do List for the White Witch. Here we might ask what Eustace likes to do with *his* time. On the first page readers are told that he likes to kill beetles and pin them on a card. He likes tormenting people as well, but only if he believes they cannot or will not strike back. In addition, we learn that Eustace, although quite bright in school, does not care much about any subject for its own sake, but only about the marks he can earn in that subject so he can ridicule anyone with a lower score.

Any list of Eustace's activities would also have to include his general rudeness, his nonstop complaining, and his constant attempt to degrade everyone and everything in a never-ending effort to enhance his own self-image. Despite the fact that the *Dawn Treader* is a beautiful ship—with perfect lines and every spar, rope, and pin lovingly made—Eustace can only keep on boasting about the ocean liners, motorboats, airplanes, and submarines found in his own world. All of Eustace's flaws and shortcomings can be traced to one source: his self-centeredness. If Eustace were to wear T-shirts with writing on them, and he does not seem the type of boy who would, he would have a whole wardrobe full of shirts that read *It's ALL about ME* in large letters across the front.

Soon after their arrival on the *Dawn Treader*, Edmund is asked to report on Eustace, who has gone to bed immediately after getting into dry clothes. "I don't think we can do anything for him," Edmund states. "It only makes him worse if you try to be nice to him."

This, according to Lewis, is where the self-centered life ends up—at a point where no one can do enough for you because no matter how much they do, they could always do more.

The narrator sums up the self-centered life perfectly when he reports, "Eustace of course would be pleased with nothing." When you are entirely centered on yourself, you never will be pleased or satisfied or content. There will always be more to want.

Bringing Narnia Home

Because of the way Eustace's parents have raised him, because of the school he has gone to, and most of all because of the patterns he has chosen to think and act in until he can no longer break free of them, it has become impossible for anyone to help him or any good thing to please him. No one can free him from his overly critical way of looking at everyone around him or from his permanently fixed focus on himself.

No one, that is, but Aslan.

And with Eustace's permission, this is exactly what he does—making everything different. After being freed from his self-centered, dragonish nature, Eustace will be a key member of the team Aslan sends to free Caspian's son, Rilian, from his years of captivity in the Underland. Then, in *The Last Battle*, Eustace and Jill together will rescue King Tirian. Given

Eustace's future roles, it could be argued that in *The Voyage of the Dawn Treader* he is saved—saved from a miserable, self-centered life—so that he can save others. Before they go to Narnia, Edmund refers to his cousin as a "record stinker." Here Lewis wants to remind his readers that the most miserable sinners, or in Eustace's case the most miserable stinkers, can become the greatest saints.

"FURTHER IN"

QUESTIONS FOR REFLECTION

1. The story of the selfish person who is finally able to become unselfish is a common one. Can you think of other storybook characters who eventually are freed from a life that is surrounded and bounded by self? What did that entail for these characters?

2. Can you think of someone you know who is overly focused on themselves? Would you say they help support Lewis's point that the self-centered life is not cool or fun and does not lead to happiness?

3. Not long after Edmund's talk with Aslan, the White Witch comes to claim him, declaring, "You have a traitor there, Aslan." Then we find

one of Lewis's most moving statements: "Of course everyone present knew that she meant Edmund. But Edmund had got past thinking about himself.... He just went on looking at Aslan." And this seems to be Aslan's goal for everyone— for us to get past thinking about ourselves. Can you think of a time when you were able to focus on someone else rather than yourself?

CHAPTER 10

THE VIRTUOUS LIFE IS A REAL ADVENTURE

Yes, One That Includes Real Hardship, but One You Don't Want to Miss

CORRECTING OUR IMAGE OF THE VIRTUOUS LIFE

Over the past century or so, the v-word has fallen out of favor. Few young people today have any interest—or think they have any interest—in a lesson about the virtues. In fact, if told that a story they were about to read was going to be about the virtuous life, most young people would go running for the hills because when they hear the v-word, most young people think one thing: *boring.*

In *The Chronicles of Narnia* C. S. Lewis intends to change this perception. Over the course of the seven books, eight different children from our world are sent to Narnia. And the experiences they have there are the total opposite of boring. Peter makes this point at the end of *Prince Caspian*, where, in typical British understatement, he exclaims, "Well! We *have* had a time."

A brief list of the adventures that Peter, Susan, Edmund, Lucy, Eustace, Jill, Digory, and Polly go on includes saving Narnia from the White Witch, taking back Caspian's crown from his usurper uncle, sailing to the end of the world in search of Narnia's seven lost lords, journeying to the Underland to rescue the missing Prince Rilian, delivering London from Queen Jadis, and rescuing King Tirian.

If, as we have seen, Lewis wants to point out that the self-centered life is not cool or fun, he also wants to say that the virtuous life—the courageous, wise, faithful, resolute, unselfish life lived by the good characters in Narnia—is not dull or dreary. The virtuous life is a real adventure.

The kind we all long for.

ALL MEANS VIRTUOUS

Before exploring Lewis's claim that the virtuous life is an adventure, we first need to understand what a virtuous life looks like. In each of the Narnia stories we find two sides in conflict: the forces of good and the forces of evil. One of the biggest differences between them is the goal each side has. The evil side wants to see Narnia enslaved, tyrannized, subjugated, and otherwise miserable. By contrast, the good side wants Narnia to be free, comforted, left alone, and happy. As each story progresses, we find that the goal each side has is not the only way they differ. They also differ just as much in the *means* that each side employs to achieve their ends.

We could sum up the difference this way. The wicked forces will use *any and all means available* to accomplish their goals. The good side can use only *all means virtuous*. Let's take a look at a few examples to see how this works.

In *Prince Caspian*, Miraz certainly has evil ends—he wants to take the crown from his brother, its rightful owner, and, once he has it, to keep it from Caspian, his nephew. Miraz is ready to use any and all means available to seize and hold on to power, including murder (of his brother), attempted murder (of Caspian), imprisonment (of those who oppose him), lies and deception (pretending he has been *asked* to take the throne), exile (of the seven lords), and even genocide (of the old Narnians).

The forces of good have to be different in both their ends *and* in their *means* to these ends. They cannot use just any means, no matter how dire the circumstances. We see this principle illustrated as Caspian, after many days of fighting and losing, convenes a meeting of his council. With the Narnian troops unlikely to survive another battle, the circumstances could hardly be more desperate. Nikabrik takes the floor and declares that their appeal for assistance from Aslan has failed, and so they must look to other powers. He has brought a Hag to the council in disguise and now plans to use her to bring back the ghost of the White Witch.

"When your sword breaks, you draw your dagger," Nikabrik declares, as though Aslan and the Witch are *both* available to him to use as he likes, and receiving help from one is just as acceptable as receiving help from the other.

Clearly Nikabrik shares Miraz's policy of using all means available—virtuous or not—to achieve his goals. Not only has he invited the Hag to summon up the spirit of the Witch, it is clear he intends to go through with his plan with or without the council's permission; he has also brought a werewolf to use, should anyone try to stop him.

Without waiting for approval, the werewolf tells the Hag to begin the process of summoning the Witch, saying, "Call her up. We are all ready. Draw the circle. Prepare the blue fire." Violence erupts, and Peter, Edmund, and Trumpkin—who have been listening outside—rush in at the last minute to save the day.

Yes, evil rulers like Miraz must be resisted and fought, not by all means available but only by all means virtuous. Even if he has a worthy goal, Caspian cannot resort to using evil means to achieve it. This would make him only *partly* different from his wicked uncle.

Another clear illustration of this principle is seen when Peter fights Miraz in single combat. There comes a moment when Miraz falls face downward, not from a blow by Peter but having tripped on an uneven patch of grass. A great shout goes up from the Narnians, but rather than rushing in to finish off his opponent, Peter takes a step back and waits for Miraz to get back up.

"Oh bother. Need he be as gentlemanly as that?" Edmund wonders. Edmund's conclusion is that yes, Peter needs to be exactly that gentlemanly, for this is what Aslan would want. If the good side is to defeat Miraz, it must be done *fairly*.

Miraz's two closest advisors, Sopespian and Glozelle, do not share Peter's scruples and are hungry for power themselves. Like the king they advise, they are more than willing to do whatever it takes to get what they want. What they happen to want is to get rid of Miraz so they can be in charge themselves. After Miraz falls, they raise a shout of "Treachery! To arms!" and in the confusion that follows, Glozelle secretly stabs Miraz—a fitting end for a wicked tyrant who came to power in a similar way using similar means.

REAL HARDSHIP AND REAL REWARDS

Earlier we looked at two kinds of stories. One kind makes us feel that our life is even less exciting than we thought. The other kind is just the opposite and leaves us feeling better about our own lives, not worse. There are also two types of stories when it comes to pain and suffering.

Fans of the first type want any story they read to be pleasant. If there is any pain or suffering, it has to be the kind that need not be taken seriously. Think of the suffering in a typical episode of *The Brady Bunch* or *Happy Days*. If there is any, it does not go very deep or last very long. Any pain is quickly over and quickly forgotten.

Lewis claims that the virtuous life is a real adventure, but he also makes it clear it will involve real pain and hardship. Compare the type of sorrow in an episode of *Happy Days* with the sorrow Susan and Lucy experience at the Stone Table after Aslan's death or with the shock and dismay Caspian feels when he learns his father was murdered by his uncle or the misery Eustace must endure when Aslan tears off his dragon skin.

The pain in Narnia hurts. It has to. Lewis would be lying to us if he suggested that a virtuous life did not also mean real hardship. This is just the way it works—in Narnia and in our own world.

Other writers might stop there (and many, in fact, do) by simply saying that life is full of agony and suffering. Not Lewis. He does show us how the virtuous life involves real hardship. But that is only part of the story. It is also the only path that can and will lead to real joy, real community, and real fulfillment.

Think of the joy Lucy and Susan experience after Aslan comes back to life and romps with them around the Stone Table. The White Witch has never known this kind of joy—not once, not for a second—and never will. Think of how happy Eustace is and the friends he has after his "un-dragoning." Even on his very best day before he came to Narnia he did not have this kind of happiness. He never even imagined such happiness existed.

One of Lewis's finest descriptions of the contentment a virtuous life offers can be found after the great feast at the end of *Prince Caspian*. There the narrator reports: "The best thing of all about this feast was that there was no breaking up or going away, but as the talk grew quieter and slower, one after another would begin to nod and finally drop off to sleep with feet towards the fire and good friends on either side."

Dropping off to sleep with feet towards the fire and good friends on either side—here is something that Miraz, who had no friends, never experienced.

Lewis has one further statement to make about

the rewards of the virtuous life—at some point the joy, community, and fulfillment will not end but will go on forever and ever. On the final page of *The Last Battle* readers are told that for those who reach Aslan's Country, all their previous life is only the cover and title page. "Now at last," Lewis writes, "they were beginning Chapter One of the Great Story which no one on earth has read: which goes on for ever: in which every chapter is better than the one before."

Every chapter is better than the one before. This, Lewis tells us, is where the virtuous life ultimately leads.

BRINGING NARNIA HOME

In *The Silver Chair*, we learn that the English boarding school where Jill and Eustace are students is called Experiment House. Lewis tells us that the teachers who run Experiment House take the overall view that boys and girls "should be allowed to do what they liked." Unfortunately, what the biggest boys and girls at Experiment House like best is bullying the others. Because of this all sorts of horrid things go on there that would have been found out and stopped at a normal school.

Aslan is a very different kind of teacher and takes a very different view. His educational philosophy could be stated as the belief that boys and girls should be encouraged to do what is best for them. And in Aslan's view what is best for them is living a virtuous life, one filled with a commitment to a greater good, rather than merely to one's self. Yes, it will include real hardship, but it is the only path that will lead to real joy, real community, and real fulfillment.

"FURTHER IN"

QUESTIONS FOR REFLECTION

1. Lewis wants to remind us—and we need this reminder again and again—where the virtuous life leads and where the self-centered life will take us. Can you think of other examples in *The Chronicles of Narnia* or in other stories where we see this illustrated?

2. Can you think of someone you know who lives the kind of virtuous life we see in the Narnia characters? Would you say that person is happy? What are some of the circumstances of his or her life that support your conclusion?

3. What might Lewis's points about the virtuous life have to do with your own life? How does one stay on course for living a virtuous life?

CHAPTER 11

ADVENTURES BEGIN IN THE MOST UNLIKELY PLACES

(Something to Keep in Mind the Next Time You're in an Unlikely Place)

ONCE THERE WERE FOUR CHILDREN

Every story must begin somewhere, but *where* and *how* it begins is one of the many important choices an author must make. If we look closely at the way Lewis chooses to begin the Narnia stories, we find that an interesting pattern emerges.

The Lion, the Witch and the Wardrobe begins during World War II with the air raids on London that cause Peter, Susan, Edmund, and Lucy to be sent to stay at the home of an old professor who lives in the heart of the country. On the first night, the siblings meet in the girls' bedroom and make plans to explore the woods around the house. But when they awake the next morning, a steady rain is falling so thick that when they look out the window they cannot see past the back garden.

Edmund, in typical early Edmund fashion, is quick to complain about the weather that has derailed their outdoor plans. Susan assures him it will clear up soon and proposes that in the meantime there is a wireless (their name for the radio) and lots of books. Peter suggests that instead they explore the house. Everyone quickly agrees, and the narrator reports, "And that was how the adventures began."

As the four children work their way through the professor's large, rambling home, they come upon a room that is totally empty except for a big wardrobe against the wall and a dead blue-bottle fly on the window sill. "Nothing there!" announces Peter, and they all troop out, except for Lucy, who stays behind in the oddly empty room to take a look inside the odd wardrobe.

And that was how the adventures began—because of a war, because of the air raids on London, because of being sent away, and because of a drenching rain.

What is Lewis saying through this beginning? First, he seems to be saying that adventures can—and typically do—begin in unexpected places and in unexpected ways. Second, Lewis also seems to be saying that negative circumstances—big and small—may be more likely to lead to great adventures than positive ones.

The start of the second story, *Prince Caspian*, follows this same pattern, as we find Peter, Susan, Edmund, and Lucy sitting on a deserted train platform, trunks and suitcases piled around them, as they wait for the trains that will take the girls to their school and the boys to theirs. It is just an empty, sleepy country station—not a place where you would expect anything amazing could begin. Again, the story opens in negative circumstances as the narrator tells us everyone feels like their "term-time" feelings are beginning again, and this makes them all "rather gloomy." And then Lucy feels a little tug, then they all do, and the next moment they are no longer in England but starting another amazing adventure.

In chapter 1 of *The Voyage of the Dawn Treader*, Edmund and Lucy are even gloomier than at the start of the previous story. Then they were only going back to school. Now they must endure a lengthy visit at Eustace's house. In *The Silver Chair*, Lewis has Jill and Eustace begin their adventure two weeks into their miserable term at Experiment House, with eleven weeks of "hopelessness" still to come.

There is just something about hopeless, gloomy circumstances, Lewis suggests, that is conducive to the start of great adventures.

DIGORY AND SHASTA

Lewis's pattern of negative circumstances serving as the gateway to adventure can be seen in the books that follow as well. At the start of *The Magician's Nephew* we meet Digory, who used to live in the country where he had a pony to ride and a river at the bottom of the garden to play in. But because his father is far away in India and his mother is sick and expected to die, they are forced to move into his mad uncle's house in London, a setting Digory refers to as a "beastly Hole." Shortly afterward he meets Polly and things begin to change, but not because the weather is so lovely they get to play outside all the time. Lewis tells us: "Their adventures began chiefly because it was one of the wettest and coldest summers there had been for years."

Perhaps of all the Chronicles, *The Horse and His Boy* begins with the most unhappy circumstances. When the story opens, Shasta, who in reality is the son of King Lune of Archenland, is living as the adopted son of a harsh and brutal Calormene who forces him to long days of backbreaking work and frequently beats him. One day a Tarkaan from the south arrives and announces he wants to buy the boy. But rather than being a turn for the good, this would be an even worse condition. Bree, the Tarkaan's horse, warns Shasta, "You'd better be lying dead tonight than go to be a human slave in his house tomorrow." And so—after years of laboring for a heartless foster father and the even worse prospect of being sold into slavery—Shasta's quest to reach Narnia with Bree begins.

There is something about negative situations like these—more so than positive ones, Lewis suggests—that can lead to new possibilities. At the end of the first book, the professor gives the children this advice about getting back to Narnia: "It'll happen when you're not looking for it." And his statement proves truer than readers might realize. We seldom see unpleasant situations as the ones most likely to lead to great adventures and as holding the greatest potential for growth.

It will be during a time when we are not looking for it and least expect it that our greatest adventures will begin.

You Must Go Alone and at Once

When Lucy and Edmund are sent to stay with their cousin Eustace at the start of *The Voyage of the Dawn Treader*, they must feel—to borrow Shasta's words—like they are the most unfortunate boy and girl that ever lived in the whole world. While Peter studies with the professor and Susan goes to America with their parents, they get stuck staying at the Scrubbs'.

But Edmund and Lucy's situation, however unpleasant, cannot compare with what happens at the start of *Prince Caspian,* when Caspian has to leave all he has ever known and flee for his life.

Caspian's adventure starts out badly, and then things get even worse. After being woken in the middle of the night and taken to the top of the Great Tower, Caspian is told that because his uncle now has a son, his life is in grave danger and he must depart or perish.

"You must go alone and at once," Doctor Cornelius explains.

Climbing upon his faithful horse, Destrier, his sword buckled beneath his cloak, Caspian leaves the castle of his ancestors and rides alone into the darkness. And what happens next could be said to have happened all because of a great knock on his head.

Night eventually gives way to a cold and rainy morning. In the dim light, Caspian threads his way through unknown woods and over wild heaths toward a line of blue mountains off in the distance. The world seems large and strange to the young traveler on his own for the first time, and he feels frightened and small. With each passing hour, the mountains grow bigger and blacker, and gradually evening begins to close in and the wind starts to rise. Soon rain is falling in torrents, and thunder is in the air. Both Caspian and Destrier are uneasy as they enter a dark pine forest that seems to go on and on.

The winds suddenly become a roaring tempest, making the woods thrash and moan. Lightning flashes right next to them, immediately followed by a great crack of thunder. Destrier bolts in panic, and it is all Caspian can do not to fall off. With his life literally hanging by a thread, the young prince tries desperately to avoid the branches that come at him in the mad dash. Almost too suddenly to hurt, something strikes Caspian on the forehead and then, we are told, "he knew no more."

If, as Lewis suggests, there is something about negative situations that can lead to new possibilities, then great opportunities should be waiting for Caspian just ahead, for his situation could hardly be more negative. And they are.

When Caspian finally comes to, he finds himself in a place he has only imagined: inside a badger's lair. Talking in lowered voices are three Old Narnians, creatures Caspian has only heard of in stories and has been longing to meet ever since he can remember. Two of them, Trumpkin and Trufflehunter, will come to be numbered among Caspian's most faithful subjects and best friends in the world. And without the threat of being killed by his uncle, an awful thunderstorm, a wild ride, and a nasty knock on the head, he never would have met them.

BRINGING NARNIA HOME

"Of course it *would* be raining!"

These are the words said by Edmund on that first morning at the professor's, the day when their great adventure had its beginning. Looking back, we can imagine what Edmund might have said if he knew what the rain was going to lead to. Perhaps something like, *"Thank goodness, it's raining!"*

While we may never travel through an enchanted wardrobe or sail on uncharted seas, Lewis suggests that we each have a journey of our own to make. There is an adventure waiting for each one of us. And if Lewis is correct, this adventure is more than likely to begin in an unlikely place and with unpleasant circumstances. Throughout the Narnia stories, Lewis reminds us that *difficult times are the soil where great adventures sprout.*

And this is something to remember the next time you find yourself facing difficult times.

"FURTHER IN"

QUESTIONS FOR REFLECTION

1. Can you think of other Narnia adventures that begin in unlikely places or unlikely ways?

2. What about in your own life? Can you think

of difficult circumstances that have led to great adventures?

3. If our encounter with *The Chronicles of Narnia* is like an adventure, one that takes us "further up and further in" each time we read, what might readers gain from this armchair adventure, the adventure of reading?

CHAPTER 12

OF COURSE HE'S NOT SAFE

(But He's Good)

WHO SAID ANYTHING ABOUT SAFE?

Today if readers look carefully at the cover of a recent edition of *The Magician's Nephew*, they will find it has a big number one on its spine, put there to tell readers that it is the first book in the *The Chronicles of Narnia*. But during C. S. Lewis's lifetime, *The Lion, the Witch and the Wardrobe* always was numbered first. The original numbering reflected the order in which the books were published. The modern renumbering was made to show their chronological order within the Narnian world. Many Lewis fans prefer the original numbering rather than the new one because reading *The Lion, the Witch and the Wardrobe* first, rather than later in the series, allows us to walk *with* Peter, Susan, Edmund, and Lucy—not *ahead* of them.

When Lucy leaves the wardrobe for the first time

and steps out into the middle of a wintery forest, she has no idea where she is—and unless we already have read *The Magician's Nephew*, neither do we. After they all make it to Narnia, the four Pevensie children gradually come to learn about the amazing land and the great lion who is its rightful ruler—and, if we are reading *The Lion, the Witch and the Wardrobe* first, we learn right along with them.

This idea of walking with the Pevensies rather than ahead of them can especially be seen in their first meeting with Mr. Beaver, in the forest near Mr. Tumnus's cave. Making signs for them to be quiet, he whispers for the children to come further into the woods, where he tells them, "They say Aslan is on the move."

At this point the narrator steps in to tell us, "None of the children knew who Aslan was any more than you do; but the moment the Beaver had spoken these words everyone felt quite different." If we start with *The Lion, the Witch and the Wardrobe*, rather than with *The Magician's Nephew,* the narrator's statement—"none of the children knew who Aslan was any more than you do"—is true, and we are able to share the children's mysterious sense of awe and wonder. As they come to know more and more about who Aslan is, so do we.

Mr. Beaver invites the children to his home in

the middle of a frozen pond where they can have a real talk. After a delicious home-cooked meal from Mrs. Beaver, Mr. Beaver pushes his chair back and announces that now they need to get down to business. He reports that Mr. Tumnus was arrested by the White Witch's police. When Peter says they must do something to save the faun who risked his own safety to save Lucy, Mr. Beaver explains that they would be no help. As the only humans in Narnia, they would immediately be recognized and arrested as well. "But now that Aslan is on the move…" he reflects.

"Oh, yes! Tell us about Aslan!" several of the children say at the same time.

Gradually the children learn that Aslan is the King of the whole wood. Now that he has arrived, not only will he save Mr. Tumnus, he will put all to right.

"Is—is he a man?" inquires Lucy.

"Aslan a man! Certainly not," Mr. Beaver replies and then explains. "Aslan is a lion—*the* Lion, the great Lion."

"Is he—quite safe?" Susan wants to know.

"Who said anything about safe?" Mr. Beaver replies. "'Course he isn't safe. But he's good."

And so our first lesson about Aslan is that he isn't safe, but he's good. At this point we must turn to a letter from Lewis's *Letters to Children* in which he responded to a class of fifth graders from Maryland who had sent him questions about the Narnia stories. "You are mistaken when you think that everything in the books 'represents' something in this world," he wrote. Lewis went on to explain:

> I did not say to myself "let us represent Jesus as He really is in our world by a Lion in Narnia:" I said "let us *suppose* that there were a land like Narnia and that the Son of God, as He became a Man in our world, became a lion there, and then imagine what would happen." If you think about it, you will see it is quite a different thing.

And so Lewis makes it clear the Narnia stories were not intended to be allegories where everything in the story represents something else. Peter is not the Apostle Peter, Edmund is not Judas, and the White Witch is not Pontius Pilate. Lucy and Susan are not Mary Magdalene and the other Mary. *The Chronicles of Narnia* are a *supposal*, a chance for us to come to see and know God and his Son from a new perspective.

Lewis does not incorporate the doctrine of the Trinity into the Narnia books. As appropriate in books written for children, he keeps things simple and so does not make a distinction between the different natures of God the Father, God the Son, and God the Holy Spirit. Any lessons we learn about Aslan may be said to be lessons about God in all three persons. And these lessons about God that we bring home from Narnia may be the most important lessons of all.

Of course he isn't safe. But he's good. With these words we are told something fundamental about Aslan's nature. While Aslan will provide protection, comfort, and consolation, he also will be a source of prodding and punishment when this is what is needed. When Aslan comes into the lives of the four children, his coming is a calling as well—a calling beyond what is comfortable, beyond what is safe, beyond what they have known and are used to, but always a calling to something good—in fact, to something better than they ever could have imagined. And this, Lewis suggests, is how God works in our own lives.

No wonder that Susan replies, in what turns out to be a huge understatement, that she is going to feel nervous when it comes time to meet Aslan.

"That you will, dearie, and no mistake," Mrs. Beaver tells her and goes on to say that "if there's anyone who can appear before Aslan without their knees knocking, they're either braver than most or else just silly."

Of course he isn't safe. But he's good.

GOOD AND TERRIBLE AT THE SAME TIME

To meet Aslan, the children must travel to the Stone Table. Even with guidance and help from Mr.

and Mrs. Beaver, it will be a demanding journey filled with danger and difficulty. When they finally arrive, Edmund will not be with them. At some point during the conversation after dinner with the Beavers, he slips away and makes his way to the castle of the White Witch, where he betrays them.

After a long day's march, the sun is sinking low in the sky and casting a soft red glow over everything. Peter, Susan, Lucy, and the Beavers come to a hill with a great open space on top. In the middle of this open hilltop, a great slab of ancient gray stone covered with strange lines and figures from an unknown language rests upon four equally ancient uprights. They have reached the Stone Table. A great crowd of Narnians stands on one side of the open meadow—majestic creatures such as centaurs and unicorns, as well as more ordinary creatures such as eagles, leopards, and dogs.

And right in the middle of them all is Aslan himself.

Then Lewis's narrator tells us, "The Beavers and the children didn't know what to do or say when they saw him. People who have not been in Narnia sometimes think that a thing cannot be good and terrible at the same time. If the children had ever thought so, they were cured of it now." Then Aslan turns to them, and the children find they cannot look at him. As the narrator reports, they go "all trembly"—a perfect description of what it feels like to encounter a being who is good and terrible—we might say *terrifying*—at the same time.

The Beavers want the children to go first. The children want the Beavers to go first.

"Susan, what about you?" whispers Peter. "Ladies first."

"No, you're the eldest," Susan whispers back.

This whispering goes on for a while until Peter finally realizes that it is up to him. Drawing the sword Father Christmas gave him the day before, he raises it to the salute. Whispering to the others to pull themselves together, he advances to the great lion.

"We have come," he tells Aslan, more "trembly" than ever.

Aslan looks at them all with great, royal, solemn eyes. When he speaks, his voice is "deep and rich," and his words have a regal tone.

"Welcome Peter, Son of Adam," Aslan says. "Welcome, Susan and Lucy, Daughters of Eve. Welcome He-Beaver and She-Beaver."

Throughout *The Chronicles of Narnia*, Lewis seeks to expand and balance our view of God. Here in the children's first meeting with Aslan, we find one of Lewis's greatest teachings. Readers who have an image of a God who is only good—as many do—need to be reminded he is not just their sweet and loving heavenly father, he is also terrifying. At the same time, those who have an image of a God who is only terrifying—as Lewis himself did as a young believer—need to be reminded that he is not just a judge who demands righteousness from us, he is good as well. Lewis's portrait of Aslan serves as an equally powerful antidote for both errors.

We see these two sides of Aslan in a particularly vivid way in the scene where Aslan returns to life after his sacrifice at the Stone Table. After a marvelous meadow romp with Susan and Lucy that ends with all three lying together panting in the grass, Aslan says to the girls, "And now to business." He explains that he is going to roar and warns them to cover their ears. When he opens his mouth, we are told that his face becomes "so terrible" that Susan and Lucy do not dare to look at it. The sisters watch as the trees in a line in front of Aslan bend like blades of grass in a meadow.

Mr. Beaver tells Susan that Aslan *isn't safe, but he's good*. We might also turn his statement around. Aslan *is good, but he isn't safe*. He is not safe if you are an evildoer, like the White Witch or King Miraz. He also is not safe if you are one of the good guys. Lewis shows us this in Jill's first meeting with Aslan at the start of *The Silver Chair*. Jill is alone and thirsty on top of a great mountain. There is a stream nearby, but there is also a great lion lying next to it.

"If you are thirsty, come and drink," the lion tells her in a deep voice.

Jill is terrified, like most people when they see Aslan for the first time, so terrified that she is almost tempted to run away from the only water available, the only thing that can quench her thirst. Jill first wants to see if the lion will promise not to do anything to her if she does come.

"I make no promise," the lion tells her.

"Do you eat girls?" she asks.

"I have swallowed up girls and boys, women and men, kings and emperors, cities and realms," he answers.

Aslan is good and terrifying at the same time. Yes, he is good, but he definitely isn't safe.

Not Like a Tame Lion

In the final chapters of *The Lion, the Witch and the Wardrobe*, the White Witch is defeated, and Peter, Susan, Edmund, and Lucy are crowned as the new kings and queens of Narnia. A great feast is held in their honor at the castle of Cair Paravel, with plenty of music, revelry, and dancing. Amidst all the jubilation, Aslan quietly slips away without saying a word to anyone. The narrator then explains how the children had been warned by Mr. Beaver that Aslan would be coming and going like this. One day they would see him, and the next he would be gone.

"He'll often drop in," Mr. Beaver had explained. "Only you mustn't press him. He's wild, you know. Not like a *tame* lion."

Here Lewis offers another important lesson about Aslan. He is not someone that anyone can control or tell what to do or how to do it. He especially will not be told *when* to do something. As Peter explains in *Prince Caspian*, "We don't know when he will act. In his time, no doubt, not ours."

He's not like a tame lion. Aslan is not someone you can put limits on. His actions are not the sort of thing you can predict. Except for knowing it will be good, we cannot say for sure what he will do, or when he will do it. *He's wild*.

Throughout the Narnia stories, various characters try to have Aslan conform to their own wishes and expectations. And when they do, Aslan makes it clear that it is *they* who must conform to *his* wishes, not the other way around. Even Lucy is partially guilty of this practice, as we discover in the scene where she meets Aslan in *Prince Caspian*. She complains to him, "I thought you'd come roaring in and frighten all the enemies away—like last time."

A chapter later, Peter makes the same mistake of

trying to limit how Aslan might act. "Why should Aslan be invisible to us?" Peter protests. "He never used to be."

Even the wardrobe seems to have a will of its own, a will that is subject to Aslan's will, not the children's. Sometimes it allows them to travel to Narnia, while at other times the way is blocked. At the end of their first adventure the Professor tells the children they cannot control when they will next get called to Narnia, nor can they predict it—we realize this is up to Aslan, not them.

"Don't *try* to get there at all," the Professor wisely tells them. "It'll happen when you're not looking for it."

Aslan's comings and goings, his decisions of when and how to intervene, and when not to intervene, are not subject to his followers' preferences. There is something about us, Lewis suggests, that wants to tell God what he should do and how he should do it. We often expect God to work in the same way he has worked before, in a way that fits our preconceived notions of how he ought to do things. We especially may feel tempted to tell God *when* he should do something and want him to act in *our* time, not his.

But being open to Aslan's plans if we are in Narnia or to God's plans in our world—*whatever they might turn out to be*—is a key component of faith. How

God works and when God works may be something we fully understand only later. Why did Aslan deliver Narnia from the White Witch after a hundred years of winter rather than after fifty, or even ten? Why did Aslan return to Narnia in time to save Caspian, but not Caspian's father? Lewis suggests that questions such as these are ones that will not or, given our limited point of view, *cannot* be explained. Aslan's actions are beyond our control and may sometimes be beyond our understanding, at least temporarily.

After Lucy says the spell that will reverse invisibility in *The Voyage of the Dawn Treader*, Aslan appears and joins Lucy and the magician, Coriakin, for a short visit. But before long, he announces that he must leave them.

"Do not look so sad," Aslan tells Lucy. "We shall meet soon again."

Lucy asks him what does he call *soon*, and Aslan tells her, "I call all times soon."

Peter's words to Caspian—"in his time, no doubt, not ours"—and Aslan's words here to Lucy suggest that there is a difference between Aslan's time and the Pevensies' time, or in our world, between God's time and our time. There is something in us that makes us think that we know when God should act, that we know what is best. There is something in us that wants God to act now, not later.

I call all times soon. In Aslan's words we can hear an echo of 2 Peter 3:9: "The Lord is not slow about His promise, as some count slowness" (NASB). We may also hear an allusion to Christ's promise from Revelation 22:20: "Yes, I am coming soon" (NIV).

Aslan is never late, though it may sometimes feel that way to those who are waiting for him. Not only is he never late, he also is not off somewhere twiddling his thumbs or attending to the needs of someone more desperate or someone more to his liking. He certainly is not being kept away by some obstacle to his acting or by some unforeseen delay. He always works in his own time, the right time—neither sooner, nor later.

So what are we supposed to do in the meantime? What is the role of those who must wait? Lewis shows us that these times of waiting are the exact thing needed to develop and deepen the virtues of faith, hope, and patience—and not just that. We do not simply wait passively. Peter tells Caspian that in the meantime, Aslan would like them to do what they can.

God's people have long cried out, "How long, O Lord, how long?" The New Testament concludes with a prayer for Jesus to come quickly, as he has promised. The Lord does, indeed, sometimes seem very slow to us. So what are we *not* to do while we wait? We are not to despair or lose hope. We are not to think we do not matter. We are not to doubt God's goodness. Lewis would add that in the meantime, we are not to try to force or trick or try to manipulate God into acting in our time not his. Not only would this be wrong, it simply will not work.

He's not a tame lion.

BRINGING NARNIA HOME

After being reunited with Aslan in *Prince Caspian*, Lucy takes a few moments to calm down and catch her breath. After she does, her first words are, "Aslan, you're bigger."

"That is because you are older," Aslan tells her.

"Not because you are?" Lucy asks.

"I am not," Aslan answers. "But every year you grow, you will find me bigger."

Aslan, you're bigger. With these words, Lewis suggests that our image of God will grow larger over time, not because God changes, but because our ability to perceive him is greater. We should note that Aslan does not tell Lucy, "Every year you will find me bigger" as though time alone will bring this larger perception. His words are, *Every year you grow, you will find me bigger.* Here Lewis warns us that growth is not automatic. It is possible to stop growing. And if we stop growing, our view of God will stop growing.

Instead of getting bigger, it will get stuck, keeping us from seeing God more and more as he truly is.

But Lewis's focus here is on Aslan's promise, on the positive, not the negative. Each year we grow, we will find God bigger—not because he has changed, but because we have. Each year we grow, we will find the God of the universe to be less safe, less tame, and more terrifying than we ever had thought. At the same time, we will find him to be more *good* than we ever had imagined.

"FURTHER IN"

QUESTIONS FOR REFLECTION

1. After Peter hears from Mr. Beaver that Aslan "isn't safe, but he's good," he replies, "I'm longing to see him, even if I do feel frightened." Lewis presents a balanced image of God, who is good and terrible at the same time. What about your own image of God? Is it too heavy on goodness and not terrifying enough? Is it too terrifying without an equal amount of goodness included?

2. Mr. Beaver tells the children that Aslan is not like a tame lion; he's wild. This is an idea Lewis returns to in *The Voyage of the Dawn Treader,* in the scene where Aslan visits Lucy and the magician. After Aslan disappears, the magician

tells Lucy, "It's always like that, you can't keep him; it's not as if he were a *tame* lion." There is a wildness to God's mercy, a wildness that may blow us right off the map that we have laid out for ourselves, a wildness that may sink all the plans we have made in ways that we never would have foreseen. Can you think of a time in your own life when you have experienced this wildness of God? Give some details.

3. C. S. Lewis intends our journey to Narnia to give us a new way to look at many things, none more important than a new way of viewing God. How has Lewis's portrait of Aslan changed the way you see God? How was Lewis's choice of a great lion a fitting way to embody God's nature?

CLOSING WORDS

At the end of *The Voyage of the Dawn Treader,* Lucy and Edmund must say goodbye to Aslan and return to England. But before they go, Lucy asks Aslan if he will tell them when they can come back to Narnia again.

"Dearest, you and your brother will never come back to Narnia," Aslan tells her gently.

Never come back to Narnia? Really? Stunned by the news, Lucy bursts into tears. "It isn't Narnia, you know," she says between sobs. "It's *you*. We shan't meet *you* there. And how can we live, never meeting you?"

But then comes the best news Lucy could ever hear.

"But you *shall* meet me, dear one," Aslan tells her, and then he explains that he is in her own world as well, but there he has a different name.

"You must learn to know me by that name," Aslan says. "This was the very reason why you were brought to Narnia, that by knowing me here for a little, you may know me better there."

And Lewis would say these same words to us. This was the very reason why we were brought to Narnia, that by knowing Aslan there for a little, we may come to know him better in our world by the name he is called here. So far we have been bringing Narnia home in the many lessons we learn there. But it turns out that the very reason for going to Narnia can be found much closer than we ever thought.

And that is the best news we could ever hear.